LIGHT

fay sweet

LIGHT

CREATIVE LIGHTING SOLUTIONS INSIDE & OUT

David & Charles

Jacket photography
front Christopher Wray Lighting
back Michael Dunn/Elizabeth Whiting Associates

A DAVID & CHARLES BOOK

First published in the UK in 2001

Copyright © Fay Sweet 2001

Fay Sweet has asserted her right to be identified as author of this work
in accordance with the Copyright, Designs and Patents Act, 1988.

A catalogue record for this book is available from the British Library.

ISBN 0 7153 1181 6

Commissioning editor   Lindsay Porter
Art editor   Ali Myer
Desk editor   Jennifer Proverbs
Text editor   Carey Denton

Printed in Hong Kong by Dai Nippon
for David & Charles
Brunel House   Newton Abbot   Devon

contents

light is life

Without light there is nothing. It's as dramatic as that. Without light there are no plants and therefore no animals. Without light, our world lacks shape and form and colour. During the past century, our lives became suffused with light and we've revelled in it. Through the visions and technical skills of modern architects our homes have been opened up to the pleasures of natural light, and for the first time in history we've had on-tap, artificial electric light which has extended our days and irrevocably changed the way in which we live.

While it is an absolute fact that we need light, I'd also suggest that we need darkness. Darkness adds modulation, contrast, subtlety, excitement, restfulness, mystery. To balance the most dramatic excesses of light, darkness is the perfect counterweight; on a hot, bright sunny day in the Mediterranean, how welcome are the cool shadows?

Light and dark are not only physical entities – they also have powerful cultural associations, both throughout the world and in the past and present. Early civilisations, including the Ancient Egyptians, worshipped the sun, and in the Bible, 'God saw the light, that it was good; and God divided the light from the darkness'. Light is so often linked with goodness, purity, spiritual cleansing and heroes, while in the netherworld of shadows there is evil lurking, and the Devil is the wicked, cruel Prince of Darkness.

It is only in recent years that we have started to understand and appreciate the real power of light and its impact on our health and our emotions. We need sunlight so that

A great lighting scheme enhances any home by shaping your living space, highlighting architectural details and giving you the flexibility to create different moods.

our bodies can produce Vitamin D, but more than that, the warmth and light of the sun's rays actually make us feel good. A sunny holiday is often prescribed as a tonic for anyone recovering from an illness. In regions including Scandinavia and Alaska, where winter is long and dark, the lack of sunlight has a tangible negative effect and is held responsible for lowering spirits and inducing depression. Seasonal Affective Disorder, also known as SAD, is recognised as a clinical illness thought to be triggered by a lack of natural sunlight, and its treatment is often with artificial light therapy.

With technological and manufacturing advances has come a whole palette of artificial lighting. To supplement natural sunlight (which, of course, also gives us moonlight), we have added humble candlelight, the common tungsten light bulb and then light sources as diverse as fluorescent, neon and halogen. With these we illuminate our environment inside and out.

Turning on an electric light bulb at the flick of a switch is certainly the easiest way of filling a space with a pool of light, but to make a room comfortable and inviting the manipulation of that precious, yet ubiquitous, commodity is one of the trickiest interior designing skills to master. It is the aim of this book to explore the phenomenon of light and to demonstrate and explain how best it can be used to enhance our home environment.

There have been any number of books published which explain the scientific composition of natural and artificial light, but here I set out to demystify the technology, quickly pass on to the creative potential of the medium and suggest how imaginative, impressive and flexible schemes can be designed and implemented. For me, the best way of understanding how to manipulate light, particularly the artificial variety, is to think like a painter. Imagine a lighting scheme as multi-layered, built up first of washes of background light which might include a central pendant, and then given more interest,

height and depth with wall lights, table lamps and tall, floor-standing lamps. All the while, remember that the quality, intensity and spread of this illumination will react with your room's colour scheme. So far we have a space filled with a fairly even spread of light. Next, for some real drama add in your points of interest, for example you can use focussed spotlights to create highlights picking up architectural detail or trained on paintings or a piece of sculpture. Where beams of light are at their most intense on a subject, there, at the edges, will we also find the densest shadows to give form to objects and underline the dramatic tension.

When you have a clear idea of the lighting effect to be achieved, you can consider the actual fittings. Today the choice is quite vast; on the one hand fittings are made as small as you like, designed to disappear almost entirely, while at the other end of the scale they can be made as huge set-pieces, decorative objects in their own right. Whatever your ideas and your taste in interior style, the design process begins with a purely objective look at the space to be transformed.

first steps

There are three key steps to assessing the lighting needs of a room. The first is to take account of the size and shape of the space: larger rooms will require more light sources than small ones to ensure an even spread of ambient light. A better quality of light is achieved if you increase the number of light sources rather than making do with just a few and giving them brighter bulbs. Also, if the room is exceptionally high- or low-ceilinged, this will need to be taken into account, as lighting can be used to create the effect of raising or lowering the ceiling. The décor and furnishings play their part too – a modern, white-painted room is likely to require quite different lighting from a more lavishly decorated space.

The second point is to be aware of the natural lightfall in the room. In broad terms, in the northern hemisphere, north and north-east facing rooms receive a cooler light than south and south-west facing rooms. The north-facing studio has always been favoured by artists because it receives more constant light with fewer variations than light pouring in from the south. Rooms facing due east will get the powerful morning sun and the evening setting sun will flood in from the west. Window treatments will have an impact on the light actually falling into the room, for example heavy curtains will block out considerably more natural light than blinds.

Natural light will always need to be supplemented by artificial lighting for dull days, dark winter mornings and evenings, but also for areas where you may be involved in intricate, close-up activities such as cooking, sewing or working at a computer. So the third key consideration is how the space is to be used and what type of moods you want to create.

A really imaginative and yet fairly simple scheme, comprising a lowered ceiling and lamps set in the large circular recesses, washes of light down the kitchen cupboard doors and the refrigerator, and unusual ceiling lamps on stems.

styles of light fitting

There's no better time to start thinking about new lighting schemes because we are now completely spoilt for choice when it comes to light fittings. Even five or ten years ago, most of the displays in regular interior design shops were certainly limited and frequently dull. However, retailers have now got the message that there is a public with a voracious appetite for exciting, unusual, sleek and even industrial style fittings. Those designs previously only available to the building and shopfitting trades are now widely sold and, as a clear indication of the growing interest in good domestic lighting, specialist shops and design companies are springing up.

Fittings fall into categories described by where they are fixed and what they do. There are the familiar pendant and wall lamps, freestanding table and floor lamps, and then track lighting. But in addition to these, we can now add a vastly expanded choice of ceiling- and wall-recessed fittings, even specially durable designs for insetting into the floor. There are countless new styles of uplighters – lights which are directed upwards and bounce light off the top of the wall and ceiling, downlighters – downward pointing to wash

The choice of light fittings on offer is truly exciting, from the stylish understated pendant on the far left to the flower-like design, centre, and the unusual table lamp, right.

walls or make beautiful pools of light on the floor, spotlights for picking out detail, and, for sheer drama, there are ever more ingenious track systems which support a whole raft of lights.

At last the clever light fittings and schemes seen in restaurants, offices and shops are within our grasp and artists and designers have been busy, too, working on small edition or one-off fittings which might be a glowing three-metre tall, basketwoven tower or an entire flock of fantasy winged light bulbs in mid-flight.

As a broad, general rule it is a good idea to include a variety of fittings in each room. A single central pendant lamp may be beautiful, but the light it casts is likely to be slightly gloomy, leaving room corners in the dark and giving faces a sunken-eyed look. A more comfortable and flattering effect is immediately achieved by adding mid-height lighting such as table lamps.

As you learn and experiment and gain confidence, you will develop a feel for when to use fixed or recessed lighting and when to use the more flexible freestanding lamps. However, before you can really start planning it's useful to have an idea of the different types of light sources available.

A tall standard lamp by John Cullen Lighting, far left, throws light upwards at the ceiling which then bounces back as a diffused glow, the lava lamp of the 1970s has been revived by Mathmos to delight a new audience, centre, and if you're looking for an eyecatcher, here's something by design company Ball that's plugged in and wildly exotic.

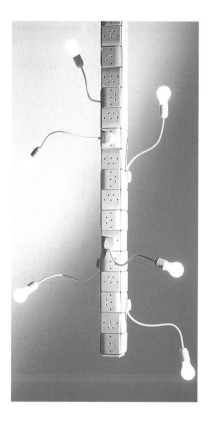

light characteristics

The good old reliable, standard, tungsten light bulb has put in remarkable service. Its warm, yellowish glow gives a soft lighting effect which remains central to most of our home lighting schemes. However, we now have the added luxury of choosing other types of illumination, the most exciting of which are the sparkling, diamond-bright halogens which began life adding a twinkle to shop window displays. But it doesn't stop there: lighting designers are making ever more interesting and creative use of neon lighting, fibre optics and coloured lighting. In addition, manufacturers are pulling out all the stops improving the quality and diversity of lighting.

To make the most of the artificial lighting at your disposal, it's useful to have a working knowledge of the different qualities of illumination:

Tungsten This is the most familiar bulb. It is available in clear, pearl or coloured glass and in the clear state offers a creamy, yellowish light. The bulbs are now produced in a huge range of shapes and sizes as well as in tubes, they are widely available and inexpensive. However, they have a relatively short life, lasting around 1000 hours.

Tungsten halogen This is fairly new on the market, and produces a nice cool, white light by using direct mains power. The small bulbs and modern light fittings are now becoming more widely available. The lifespan is at least double that of a regular tungsten bulb, but they do tend to be expensive.

Low-voltage tungsten halogen A real sparkling success, snapped up by anyone wanting to add fresh, crystalline light to their home. The drawbacks are that the bulbs are expensive and rarely sold in a local hardware

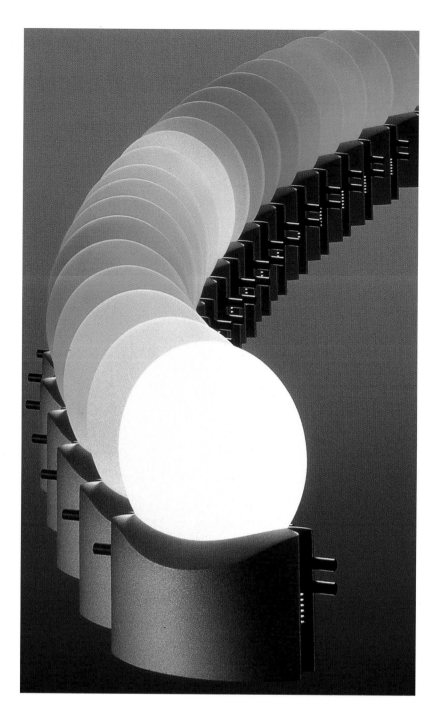

Don't restrict yourself to using just standard clear or pearlescent light bulbs; to create different effects, experiment with different colours of bulb and lampshade.

store, but also that fittings include hefty transformers to convert the mains supply for their use. They can make an annoying hum if used with dimmer switches. However, the lamps have a really long life, up to 3500 hours.

Fluorescent These used to be everyone's idea of nightmare lighting. But in recent years the technology has improved enormously to make lights that are kinder on the eye, compact and energy efficient.

planning

Armed with notes about the types of light sources you'd like to incorporate in your envisaged scheme, ideas about the styles of fittings and the varying moods you want to create, next comes the design and planning stage.

Start with the basics. I'd suggest making a floor plan, (a bird's eye view, looking down on the room), so that you can mark out where the main items – beds, tables, bath, cupboards and so on – will be placed. Make a note of any windows and which way they face so that you know when and where sunlight is coming from – huge east-facing windows in a bedroom may require heavy curtains or blinds to reduce early morning sun. Consider when the room is most used. A galley kitchen with little natural sunlight will have entirely different lighting needs from a large, open-plan kitchen/dining room flooded with light. Whatever their orientation, all rooms require general or ambient lighting: a pendant, some ceiling recessed fittings or perhaps a couple of wall lights to give background illumination. Once this is drawn onto your plan the real fun can start.

Having covered the practical considerations of sufficient background light, you can now be entirely frivolous and creative. Inspired by ideas in this book, think about incorporating more unusual lighting features in your design. Consider using lights inset into floors or treads on stairs, at the bottom of walls, behind panels of coloured glass set into the wall, at the top of cupboards, inset into the underside of shelves or perhaps a floating light raft suspended from the ceiling.

Artificial lighting adds immeasurably to the enjoyment of your home. This scheme echoes the charm of the building, marking out the entrance and the route up the spiral stair to the roof terrace.

practical details

O nce plans start to take shape it's important to think practically – is your existing electrical system in good shape? This is certainly the right time to invest in a system health check. I'd strongly recommend enlisting the help of professionals. In most countries, for a modest fee, the electrical utility companies will carry out an appraisal of your wiring. They may also be able to supply electricians to upgrade the system and install your new lighting scheme. Please note that in some countries it is illegal for householders to undertake their own electrical wiring maintenance.

Light and water are absolute winners, but remember to follow all safety procedures and precautions when fitting and using such features.

You may also elect to employ a specialist lighting designer. While this book is intended to look at and explore many aspects of lighting design and to provide plenty of inspiration, it is not a technical handbook. Once you have formulated your ideas, you may decide that you do not want to take on such a project yourself, and feel that it is well worth the investment bringing in an expert who will take on the whole job to translate your plans and ideas into reality. If possible, ask to see a couple of their previous projects and try and speak to previous clients. Along with any major works on the home, lighting design and installation can be highly disruptive and may be quite intrusive, so you need to get on with your designer and feel confident that he or she is doing a great job.

However you choose to go ahead, think well in advance about your budget. Good, well constructed and safely fitted lighting schemes are not cheap. If financially possible, it makes sense to work on an entire house or apartment in one job, rather than taking a piecemeal, room-at-a-time approach. Always get at least three quotes for the project so that you know exactly what you are paying for and are reassured that you're getting the best value for money.

Strips of tiny bulbs are charming and certainly add interest to a flight of steps, but they also have their practical aspects.

arriving

THE OLD SAYING ABOUT THE IMPACT of first impressions is as true today as ever, and so the entrance to every home speaks volumes about its occupants and the spaces inside. A front door may be flanked by hanging baskets and carriage lamps or enhanced by a terracotta pot and bay tree lit by recessed low-voltage halogen lamps. Such details offer clues and set up expectations about who and what is on the other side of the door. While the style and decoration of the entrance is a public expression of our personality, its practical purpose is to mark the line between the public space of the street and the private space of the home. The line is understood and respected by just about everyone; even regular house visitors such as the postman will not cross the threshold unless invited to do so.

The entrance, then, must perform a number of functions. It is a place where we can stamp our character, where we accept deliveries and where we greet and welcome guests. Its other vital duty is to provide us with secure protection from unwelcome visitors. In all of these guises, lighting can play an important role, whether it is in enhancing the sense of arrival or deterring any attempt to make a forced entry.

assessing needs

CHECKLIST

Providing a warm welcome is just one aspect to consider when designing and decorating an entrance way. To help you plan a lighting scheme, look to see if the following criteria are met.

■ IS THE NUMBER OR NAME OF THE HOUSE ADEQUATELY LIT?

■ IS THERE A LONG PATH OR CORRIDOR FROM THE STREET TO THE ENTRANCE. IF SO, IS IT VERY DARK AT NIGHT?

■ DO YOU PLAN TO INSTALL A SECURITY LIGHT SYSTEM?

■ DOES THE FRONT DOOR RECEIVE STREET LIGHTING?

■ CAN YOU SEE THE KEYHOLE CLEARLY IN THE DARK?

■ IF YOU HAVE A VIDEO SECURITY SYSTEM OR PEEPHOLE IN THE DOOR, CAN YOU ALWAYS SEE VISITORS' FACES CLEARLY?

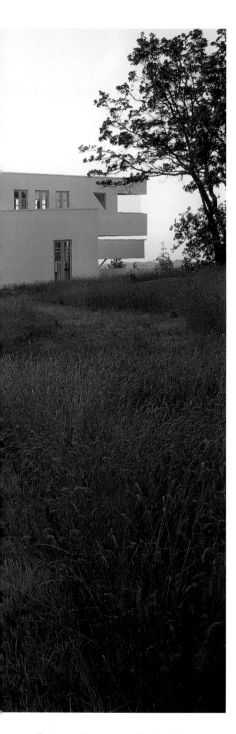

Enhance the sense of arrival by installing a dramatic lighting scheme. Here neat, domed, ground-level lamps flank the curving pathway.

T o guide night-time visitors towards the entrance and ensure they are made to feel welcome, the lighting plan begins where the public realm ends. For example, in a village where lighting of public pathways and streets is likely to be low or non-existent, a higher level of external illumination will be required than if the home is on a city street and benefits from street lamps. The first task of a lighting scheme is to indicate the name and/or number of the property. Since most homes have the number or name of the house on the door, a simple exterior wall-fixed lamp should illuminate it. If the entrance is a long way from a public path or road, an illuminated sign at the junction will be helpful.

the lighting plan

Consider the route from public land to the entrance. A short path leading to the door of a town house is likely to receive sufficient street lighting not to warrant any extra lamps, but if there are patches of darkness, lots of plant growth or dark corridors, it is a courtesy to your visitors, and helpful for you, to provide illumination for their safety and well-being. A long path can be lit by tall freestanding lamps or illuminated bollards. Where the path runs alongside a wall, lamps can be fixed to this to light the way. Security lighting, activated by heat or movement, is adequate for this job, but for a more consistent lightfall it is worth considering a separate system of path illumination. Take care to provide lighting for steps and, if you have your own parking area, light the route from the garage or parking space to the entrance.

The final stage is to design lighting for the doorway itself. A modest scheme might include a lamp suspended over the door with perhaps just one further light source at the side closest to the locks to make it easy to find the keyhole

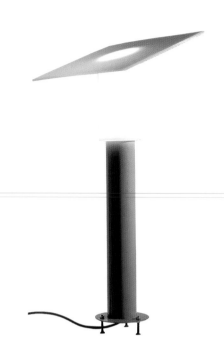

in the dark. More complex schemes might include ground-level, upward-facing spots lighting either side of the doorway to add a sense of drama and grandeur. A pair of eye-level lamps flanking the door makes a well-balanced scheme, and, if you have a video entry system, you might consider an additional lamp to illuminate the faces of callers to make them easy to recognise. With the exception of security lighting, the entrance lighting scheme should incorporate lamps that cast a soft and flattering light. This will provide a warm and welcoming atmosphere for residents and visitors alike, while still being practical. Very bright light sources will make visitors feel uncomfortable and unwelcome, and may even prove a hazard by dazzling passing motorists.

An intriguing exterior light called Outside, designed by Sebastian Bergne and made by Flos.

energy conservation

Because your exterior lighting scheme is likely to be operable for long hours at a time, consider using low-energy light bulbs. The choice is now vast and even the colouring of these low-energy sources has improved in recent years, swapping insipid, harsh lighting for a quality of light that is a lot more pleasing and comfortable on the eye.

security lighting

It is advisable to employ the services of an accredited professional when installing an exterior security lighting system. They will have information about the regulations for cabling and fittings suitable for exterior use. They should also advise on installing a system which operates independently from any other lighting at the entrance and which is difficult for intruders to disable.

A recessed, finned steplight suitable for low-level illumination and pathway lighting, which uses a 12v capsule G4 10–20w max lamp. It contains a fixed sandblasted glass lens which softens and diffuses the light. The interior version is made of cast aluminium while the exterior version is made of solid gunmetal and comes in a variety of finishes – white, black, nickel and aluminium. From John Cullen Lighting.

practicalities

Along with providing a safe and inviting welcome for your guests, it is important that the entrance lighting scheme will work for you and your family, too. This involves considerable planning and thought about how the system will actually function. Consider using a timer or switch that is activated at

dusk, so that if you have been out at work or away from the house for a while, the lighting comes on before you arrive home in the dark. This is not only a practical measure, but adds to your home's security. If you have a scheme involving a number of light sources, the timer doesn't have to switch on everything at once. You could choose to have just a basic system operated by a timer and then additional lighting which is controlled from inside. Some lights, such as one used to illuminate a house number or name board, can be conveniently left on all the time.

It is also important to have access to light switches in the garage, making it possible to control the lighting manually on the way to the house. This also helps individuals to move between the two areas safely and comfortably.

The combination of good lighting and interesting materials makes a warm welcome at this beach house, by John Wardle Architects. The rooms become glowing boxes and light fittings at the deck entrance area emphasise the rich colour and texture.

bright ideas

Lighting plans with an unusual twist are certainly the most memorable and exciting, and with entrances there is great scope for exuberance. When designing your scheme, think about the whole idea and experience of entrances and arrival, the sense of expectation, the anticipation of a warm welcome. Borrow designs from the arrival at an airport for example, with a strip of lights inset along the centre or to one side of your path leading up to the front door. Or use the idea of making an entrance Hollywood-style – start with dramatic pools of light cast down over the threshold, or beams of light washing up the face of the entrance. If there are steps leading up to the door, perhaps consider setting lights into the risers, or fixing lights at the side that wash light across the treads.

An exotic and theatrical scheme has been created for this entrance, where reflections of light in the pool heighten the impact and drama.

For those who really want to make an entrance, here's a dramatic scheme using a pair of monumental marble pillars pulled forward slightly from the exterior wall and lit from ground level behind. The light is reflected back on to the pink wall. By framing the entrance in this way, the internal view is also framed and the eye is drawn into the inner courtyard with its small garden.

Lighting the point of arrival to a home is your first offer of hospitality. Make it clear to guests which route to follow and where they must go. In this example, there's no mistaking the front door flanked by its pair of wall lights and protected from the worst weather with a small porch. The night-time lighting is given additional interest by being reflected in the small circular pool.

This is an entrance which explores the possibilities of light combined with a restrained palette of materials. It is also a vivid demonstration of the power of a simple but effective lighting plan.

This sheltered entrance is a modern interpretation of the porch: the covered area provides visitors with a space protected from the extremes of the weather where they can prepare themselves to meet their hosts. Natural light is drawn into the area through the rectangular openings made in the porch ceiling over the gravel. A sense of serenity is achieved by the plain white paintwork, the neat, central, stone-flagged pathway and the areas of raked gravel at either side of the porch. There is a framed view of the water and garden beyond.

❶ CEILING-RECESSED, WEATHERPROOF TUNGSTEN LIGHT FITTING ❷ KNEE-HEIGHT GARDEN BOLLARD WITH DOMED CAP COVER TO FOCUS LIGHTFALL DOWNWARDS ❸ RECTANGULAR LIGHT BOXES IN PORCH ROOF TO ALLOW NATURAL LIGHT TO FALL THROUGH TO THE ENTRANCE BELOW

The central feature is, of course, the large ceiling-recessed light fittings running along the spine of the covered walkway. Because they are exposed to external temperatures and weather, fittings must be chosen which are weatherproof. The tungsten lamps cast a line of warm, creamy-coloured light along the pathway, making it clear where visitors should head. The most intense pool of light is focussed on the two shallow steps which lead to the entrance door; the brightness of the light not only makes it safe to negotiate the steps but also underlines where the entrance is.

The second interesting light element is the garden bollard which provides a point of focus, drawing the eye to the garden while also providing practical lightfall to illuminate the path close to the water's edge.

circu

circulating

ONCE THE THRESHOLD HAS BEEN CROSSED, the point of arrival and departure is usually the hall. Very often nowadays it is one of the least exciting spaces in the home, a Cinderella area with simple, durable decoration, and perhaps a bookcase or a few pictures on display.

The hall has fallen on hard times and declined dramatically in importance since its heyday in the medieval era when, in Northern Europe, a hall was central to every house of substance. Here, the large room was the very hub of the home where guests were received, fed, entertained and even bedded down for the night. During the ensuing centuries, the hall was divided into separate rooms, each with its own distinct function, leaving the room we now call the hall relegated to the small lobby area around the front, and, sometimes also, the back door.

In contemporary houses the hall forms the hub of circulation space around the home and flows into the stairs and corridors, linking together different spaces. Despite the fact that this circulation space is often given low priority in decorating schemes, it provides a great opportunity for visual impact. What could be more exciting than a long narrow hall with a stunning full-height painting or pair of urns on stands at one end; a flight of stairs bathed in light from above; corridors lined with paintings or bookshelves from floor to ceiling? All of this drama is intensified one-hundredfold by bold lighting that highlights details and entices guests inside to explore and enjoy the home.

assessing needs

CHECKLIST

The shapes and dimensions of halls and corridors inevitably vary enormously, but the following questions should help you to create more imaginative lighting schemes.

■ CAN YOU ENHANCE THE NATURAL DAYLIGHT BY ADDING MIRRORS OR ADDITIONAL WINDOWS?

■ IS THIS AREA DECORATED IN LIGHT OR DARK COLOURS? DO YOU PLAN TO CHANGE THE SCHEME?

■ IS IT FURNISHED WITH BRIGHT, REFLECTIVE SURFACES SUCH AS MARBLE, VARNISHED WOOD, CERAMIC TILES AND SO ON? IF SO, YOU WILL PROBABLY REQUIRE LOWER LIGHT LEVELS THAN IN A HALL PAINTED RICH, MATT COLOURS.

■ IS THE SPACE LARGE ENOUGH FOR A DRAMATIC ADDITION SUCH AS AN ENTIRE WALL OF SHELVES, A HUGE PAINTING, OR FLOOR TO CEILING GOLD LEAF?

The main role of lighting in a hall and circulation space is to be functional; to make sure people can move around the home comfortably and safely. Areas such as stairways should be especially well lit. However, its decorative potential should not be ignored, bringing with it the chance to bring out the best in unusual dimensions and unexpected corners.

the lighting plan

It sets the scene to mark an entrance with a light that makes a statement, something that helps establish the tone for the whole home – a large lantern with coloured glass, for example. Long halls can be lit in a number of ways: for great drama, recessed fittings set in the centre of the ceiling look stunning as they cast their pools of light along the length of the hall floor. Recessed lamps fitted into the floor, reminiscent of airport runway lights, are more unusual and look equally amazing.

Wall lights can work well on their own or can be added to supplement ceiling fittings. Choose discreet uplighters to wash the upper part of the wall and ceiling or make a bold statement with original and unusual fittings. Flaming torches, illuminated horns or striking sculptural pieces may be all you need to dress an otherwise neutral space, acting both as a light source and as a focal point.

The primary task of lighting in hallways is to make circulation safe and easy. The effect is enhanced when distant lighting also draws you through the space. Here ceiling-recessed, low-voltage halogen lamps illuminate the sunshine yellow hall, while intense lights deeper into the apartment entice you to explore further.

A recessed, directional downlight called a Sputnik from John Cullen Lighting. The picture shows the importance of having sufficient space above the ceiling, approximately 120mm, for the recessed part of the fitting.

Another sort of recessed lamp, again from John Cullen Lighting, but this time inset into the floor. It is ideal for uplighting walls and architectural details such as columns and arches.

Directional downlighters in halls and corridors are effective in making an interesting scheme, too – choose ceiling-recessed lamps with an eyeball fitting or ceiling-mounted adjustable spots to wash a wall entirely hung with paintings or fitted with bookshelves.

Stairs should be lit with safety in mind. Be careful to place lights so that the lightfall is directly downwards or bounced off the ceiling – avoid any chance of bright light dazzling anyone moving up or down the stairs. Make sure that the light is brightest at the top and bottom; of each flight of stairs and that there is light on each landing. Pay particular attention, too, to the route from bedrooms to the bathroom; it is often a good idea during the night to include low-level or dimmable lighting which is permanently switched on. There are systems currently available that are activated by anyone walking to and from the bathroom and which then switch off automatically.

practicalities

Because halls and stairs and corridors tend to be narrow and are used primarily for moving around the space, these are not ideal areas for floor or table lamps. Trailing flex can be extremely dangerous.

Where the stairs do not receive natural light, in a basement for example, consider adding low-level recessed light fittings at either side of the base of the treads to cast an interesting ankle-level wash of light across the steps. If the stairwell is very dark, it is often possible to introduce an interesting shaft of natural light by inserting a 'sun pipe' into the roof. These inexpensive pipes are self-explanatory – they run between ceiling and roof and are finished on the outside with a domed cap of glass which allows light to fall into the home below.

Even where a hall is narrow, it's useful to hang or fix a mirror to check how you look before leaving the house and also to reflect light around the space. To boost light levels further, consider adding lighting above or on either side of the mirror.

Generous natural lightfall illuminates this hallway during the daytime, while artificial lighting recreates the drama at night. The darker area around this short flight of steps is illuminated by the neat, rectangular, inset, flush-fitted lamps in the stair risers.

bright ideas

Because circulation spaces need to be highly functional, offering safe passage through the house, special lighting treatments can be used as a key part of the decoration. A good lighting scheme will draw the eye through the space and invite you further inside. Along with the more usual treatments of pendant lamps and ceiling-recessed fittings, think about sculpting the space, highlighting details or adding points of interest along the route. Once again the airport runway offers inspiration – instead of, or in addition to, fitting lights into the ceiling, think about setting them in the floor. Paint the ceiling gold, silver or blue with stars and illuminate it with uplights fixed high on the walls, inset panels of sandblasted glass in the floor or wall with back illumination for an intriguing glowing effect, or carve a niche in the wall for a vase of flowers with a tiny spotlight above.

An ellipse-shaped window has been punched through this ceiling and given a double-glazed glass cover to draw natural sunlight in through the roof and then down through the floors below. Artificial lighting is fitted into the rim on the roof light and made flush with its walls. A single ordinary tungsten light bulb is used inside each recessed fitting and the light it casts adds interest at night as the eye is drawn upward through the space. The shape of the roof light is mirrored exactly in the glass-balustraded lightwell below.

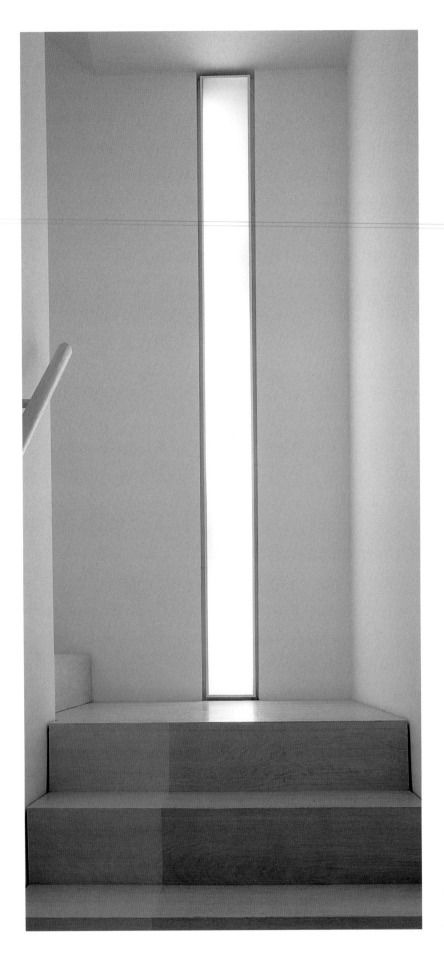

A narrow light, sunk into the wall and running from floor to ceiling, provides an illuminated column, vaguely reminiscent of arrow slits made in the sides of fortified buildings. The light tube sits inside a metal frame which holds the translucent glass panel. The obscured quality of the glass diffuses the light cast over the smooth, silky finish of the stairs and walls.

Artificial light is often deployed to give depth and form to a space. Here an unusual floor-recessed light fitting marks the threshold between the hallway and the living area, but your eye is drawn onwards to the centre of the room and its red wall, vibrant in the intense beam of a spotlight, and then onwards again to the distance and the sunlight outdoors.

An imaginative lighting scheme can help the gloomiest hall and stairway but in this particular project the generous, open stairway and landing is already a beautiful space. The lighting has been carefully chosen to make the most of its features.

It is clear that natural light is encouraged into and through the space; the glass-panelled balustrading opens up the entire room and enables light to flow down the stairwell. The space would have an entirely different feel if this balustrade were made using solid panels, or if it were painted a darker colour. The central feature is the delicate string of lights suspended from the open timber rafters through the central stairwell. These unusual and pretty lights, like falling petals or butterflies, have tiny shades facing in random directions that draw the eye upwards to accentuate the height of the space. They make a visual connection between the upper and lower levels and provide an appealing sparkle of light reflected off the glass panels. It is an inspired choice of light fitting.

Providing general illumination in this hall and over the stairway are low-voltage wall lights. The design satisfyingly positions the stepped lights to follow the exact rake of the stairs. Here is an example of practical lights providing sufficient illumination for people to move safely up and down the stairs. The same wall light fittings continue along the corridor, leading to the bedrooms.

And finally, the simple finishes of this open and airy space are softened by the addition of a huge potted ornamental plant highlighted by a small, low-voltage spotlight.

❶ AN UNUSUAL VERTICAL TRACK OF LOW-VOLTAGE HALOGEN LAMPS, HELD IN PLACE TOP AND BOTTOM WITH TENSION WIRES

❷ CONTEMPORARY-STYLE WALL LIGHTS WITH LOW-VOLTAGE HALOGEN BULBS

❸ LOW-VOLTAGE HALOGEN SPOTLIGHT ON A SHORT TRACK WITH REFLECTOR

One of the great skills in planning a lighting design scheme for a circulation area is to achieve the effect of leading the eye through the space. And in addition to creating visual interest with light, it is equally important to ensure that there is sufficient artificial or natural light to negotiate the route through the space safely.

In this example, attention is immediately drawn to the beauty and texture of the natural stone steps, which are enhanced by lighting recessed into the solid, wall side of the staircase. Fully recessed, circular, low-glare, low-voltage halogen fittings are used to skim across the face of the treads. Not only does this choice of lighting create atmosphere and interest in an area not usually treated in this manner, but it illuminates the steps for safe passage. Providing a point of interest at the top of the flight of stairs and drawing the eye up is the spotlight highlighting the handsome stone bust. This is a particularly clever piece of lighting using a fully concealed framing projector fitting, which provides a beam of light exactly to the dimensions of its subject. The concluding part of the scheme is the pair of lights providing matching scallop-shaped washes down the face of the gold-coloured doors, just picking out the delicate texture of the gold leaf. This light not only marks the end of this particular vista, but also sets up anticipation for the start of the next. Intriguingly, all will be revealed once the doors have been thrown open.

❶ FOUR MONSOON, FULLY-RECESSED, LOW-GLARE, LOW-VOLTAGE HALOGEN FITTINGS ❷ A FULLY CONCEALED, LOW-VOLTAGE HALOGEN FRAMING PROJECTOR LIGHTS THE STONE BUST ❸ A PAIR OF LOW-VOLTAGE HALOGEN SPOTLIGHTS PROVIDE SCALLOPS OF LIGHT DOWN THE DOORS. ALL FITTINGS FROM JOHN CULLEN LIGHTING

living

THE LIVING ROOM HAS BECOME ONE of the most intensely used spaces in the home, and a place that must undergo numerous character changes during the day to meet the demands of everyone who visits it. From first thing in the morning, when it may be used for watching children's television or catching up on the breakfast news headlines, to the evening, when it may double up as a dining area for entertaining friends, our living space has to be flexible and adaptable.

Today's living room has evolved from a number of rooms. A century ago the living space in a modestly appointed family home comprised a best parlour for guests and a back parlour for everyday family use, a study, a dining room and perhaps even a music room. As a result of the visionary designs by 20th century architects such as the American Frank Lloyd Wright, the constraining walls of formal living were pulled down and in their stead was provided informal, open-plan space where the whole family could share life together. The idea reached a peak in the 1960s and 70s when, even in older homes, rooms were knocked together to produce the desired open-plan effect. The concept was reinvented once again in the loft-living explosion of the 1990s where, in the most extreme cases, just about every wall in the entire home was removed to make open, light-filled, free-flowing spaces. Because the living room has to be so many things to so many people, it presents one of the greatest lighting design challenges in the home.

assessing needs

CHECKLIST

Because the living room is such a multi-functional space, its lighting scheme has to be versatile and hard working. The following questions may help you assess whether all your requirements are being met:

■ IS IT A FORMAL ROOM USED MOSTLY IN THE EVENINGS, OR AN INFORMAL, FAMILY ROOM IN USE ALL DAY?

■ IS THERE A TELEVISION AND/OR MUSIC SYSTEM?

■ DOES IT INCORPORATE A HOME OFFICE?

■ IS THERE A DINING AREA?

■ IS THE DECOR GENERALLY LIGHT OR DARK IN TONE? DO YOU PLAN TO CHANGE THE SCHEME?

■ DOES IT RECEIVE GENEROUS SUNLIGHT?

■ IS THE FURNITURE LIKELY TO STAY IN THE SAME PLACE?

■ DO YOU SPEND TIME HERE READING OR DOING OTHER CLOSE-UP WORK SUCH AS SEWING?

■ IS THE SPACE LARGE ENOUGH TO DIVIDE INTO AREAS DESIGNATED TO SPECIFIC ACTIVITIES?

There is no set formula for designing any lighting scheme, but because it is often so intensely used, the living room incorporates just about every type of lighting discussed in this book. As a starting point, assess the space, natural lightfall and décor. This is likely to be the largest room in the home and so you should anticipate the need for more light sources than anywhere else. It is perfectly feasible for some areas to be lit brightly, around a home office for example, and some to be lit by just a single lamp. If the room can be divided easily into different areas of activity, bear that in mind when thinking of a lighting plan and, for ease on the eye, vary light levels around the room. Because living rooms are used more in the evening than in the daytime, natural lightfall is not all-important. However, if the room includes a home office or somewhere for children to do their homework, then that area should be well lit with general ambient lighting such as pendant or wall lights, plus a task lamp such as a desk lamp, preferably one that can be angled so that light will fall directly where it is required. A light directed towards a bookshelf is helpful for finding titles and also makes a feature. Equally important is the provision of a reading lamp by one of the soft chairs – even in daytime, it sometimes helps to have artificial light to boost levels when reading small print.

The colour of your decorative scheme will inevitably have some effect on the lighting plan. As a general rule, a pale scheme will require slightly fewer fittings and lamps than would be the case in a darker-coloured room.

the lighting plan

Any plan should begin with general or ambient lighting – choose pendant lights or perhaps ceiling-recessed fittings which fill the room with a background wash of light. Ceiling-recessed lights incorporating an eyeball fitting give the flexibility of directional beams either pointing directly downwards or angled as wall washers. This ambient lighting scheme can be boosted and given warmth with wall lights or, if you prefer,

This extraordinary light fitting by artist Jo Whiting in collaboration with architect Simon Foxall makes a striking centrepiece for this elegant living room. It is composed of thousands of paper-thin ceramic strips and lit with ordinary tungsten lightbulbs. The chandelier casts a soft, diffused light and, by lowering the ceiling, adds a sense of intimacy.

floor-standing standard lamps which, depending on their design, will throw light down, up or across the walls. Then table lamps can be used to cast light around the lower level of the room. In addition, extra interest can be added with lamps that sit on the floor – recent intriguing designs have included a huge pebble shape in plastic, which emits a soft glow when switched on. The warmth of tungsten light bulbs works well in living spaces, with zest added by halogen bulbs in spotlights to illuminate paintings or other special objects

VISUAL TRICKS

● IF THE ROOM IS VERY TALL AND
YOU WANT TO ACCENTUATE ITS
HEIGHT, BUILD IN UPLIGHTERS TO
WASH THE CEILINGS.

● TO ACHIEVE THE EFFECT OF
LOWERING THE CEILING, INCLUDE
PENDANT LAMPS THAT CAST A
DOWNWARD LIGHT. PAINTING THE
CEILING A DARKER SHADE WILL
ALSO HELP.

● A LOW-CEILINGED ROOM CAN BE
MADE TO APPEAR HIGHER BY KEEP-
ING FURNITURE AND PICTURES AT A
FAIRLY LOW LEVEL AND THEN WASHING
WALLS AND CEILING WITH UPLIGHTERS.

● AVOID PENDANT LIGHTS IN A
LOW-CEILINGED ROOM. FOR AN
ILLUSION OF GREATER HEIGHT USE
CEILING-RECESSED FITTINGS, WALL
LIGHTS OR FREESTANDING
FLOOR LAMPS.

● CONCEALED STRIPLIGHTING FIXED
ON THE TOP OF CUPBOARDS OR
BOOKCASES IS A VERY EFFECTIVE
WAY OF CASTING LIGHT ONTO A
CEILING, WHICH IS THEN REFLECTED
SOFTLY DOWN INTO THE ROOM.

● TO MAKE A SMALL ROOM FEEL
LARGER, DECORATE USING PALE
COLOURS AND BATHE WALLS AND
CEILING GENEROUSLY WITH
ARTIFICIAL LIGHT.

● THE BEST WAY TO LIGHT
PAINTINGS AND THE TELEVISION SET
WITHOUT GLARE IS TO PLACE THE
LIGHT SOURCES ANGLED FROM
THE SIDE OF THE FLAT PLANE.

Making the most of what was a dark basement room, an entire floor has been removed to let in natural light through the main street-level window. In addition to sunlight, neat ceiling-recessed fittings provide light in the circulating space to the left while industrial-style, upward-facing flood-lights wash the wall and highlight the rich brick texture.

and to pick out architectural detailing such as a decorative cornice or industrial pipework. Make a feature of an alcove with a recessed halogen lamp, or add sizzle to glass shelving with halogen lamps fitted above or below.

practicalities

If your living room area is a generous size, and is a multi-functional room, the lighting plan is crucial to making the most of the space. I hope this book will inspire and equip you to design your own schemes. However, for something really specialized, it is worth hiring a professional lighting designer who can help you to work out ways of incorporating several lighting circuits, with separate ones for ceiling lights, wall lights, floor and table lamps, and so on. Put each circuit on a dimmer switch for maximum control.

Incorporate floor sockets so that the flex from lamps in the centre of the room doesn't trail across the floor. Add plenty of extra sockets around the skirting board for additional lamps. This means greater flexibility, so that when you move furniture you will also be able to move lamps.

If you do opt for a professional lighting designer, investigate the possibility of building in a control board with pre-set lighting programmes for different lighting moods and striking special effects.

lighting a home office area

Natural daylight is the ideal light in which to work, but, of course, is not always possible to achieve. Where a home office is incorporated into a living space, try to locate it near the window to gain some natural lightfall on the desk. If this proves impossible, make sure the work area has its own high-level lighting as we need the stimulation of brighter light to work more effectively. Artificial lighting can also be used to help mark the boundary between the desk and the rest of the room. Include a pendant lamp or wall light for ambient lighting and at least one task light, preferably an adjustable lamp, on the worktop. Ideally, separate switches from those for the rest of the living room should control the lighting in this area (see *Working* for more details).

bright ideas

In an area like a living room there are tremendous opportunities to use lighting in many different ways – for general ambient illumination of course, but also to provide a focal point, to mark out different areas and as an interior landscaping tool. Huge and unusual fittings either suspended from the ceiling or standing on the floor become intriguing sculptural elements in the room, while a sense of formality and order can be achieved when using two or more fittings of the same design – for example, a pair of standard lamps will stand sentry at either end of a sofa. The landscaping potential is under-explored in most homes; since we spend most of the time in a living area sitting down, interest can be created around the lower level of the room with floor-level and low-level lighting – with this in mind, small lamps are now made to sit on the floor. Switch off the main lights, switch on the floor lamps and the room instantly has a more intimate and restful atmosphere.

There is always something exciting about profusion. It's a sign of lavishness and generosity. In this case tiny candles, known as tea lights or night lights, are arranged in a random but dense pattern on a hearth. It is entirely appropriate to place these tiny flames at the focus of the room, the fireplace, where a live fire will be lit on cold nights. The slight movement and flicker of the flames add life to the room. Scented candles will add yet another dimension to your experience and enjoyment of a space used to relax in.

Interesting lighting schemes are created when light sources are placed at different heights in a room. This contemporary, wire-stemmed floor light with its broad-rimmed shade provides a light source at seating level. Light fittings at different levels can be used to landscape the interior. Lamps on the floor or at this low level in the room can produce a cosy and relaxed atmosphere. Lighting also has an effect on how we perceive the proportions of the room – low-level lighting makes ceilings appear much higher than they are in reality.

Pairs of lights are always a good
idea in creating a balanced lighting
scheme. Here two handsome floor-
standing lamps called Alta Costura by
the Spanish designer Josep Aregall
have been placed like sentries
on guard at each end of a sofa.
Wrapped around a long lighting tube,
the shades are made of furls of waxy
paper which cast a soft, diffused light.
And the lamps are striking to look at
even when they are switched off.

A jolly pyramid of glowing globes. This unusual and eye-catching lamp design is exactly the sort of feature that can transform an unexciting space. It is a particularly good idea to place such a lamp in an alcove or disused fireplace so that it is 'framed' and becomes a focus of the room. The additionally smart idea here has been to place a mirror in the back of this redundant fireplace, allowing some of the light to be reflected back into the room.

In this open-plan living space a flexible lighting scheme helps to divide the room into several different zones of use. To start in the centre, the fireplace is given emphasis with the pair of up-facing wall lights balanced by the downwash of the picture light. For gentle moods, there are candlesticks on the mantelpiece. Also in this area there are two unusual, floor-standing, contemporary-style standard lamps. Just out of the picture, ceiling-recessed low-voltage halogen lamps provide additional lighting above the armchair and sofa.

The dining area is lit simply with the elegant pendant lamp on a dimmer switch. Its broad glass rim is a design device for spreading the light horizontally across walls and down the neat Venetian blinds. The lighting for the home office is appropriately bright and efficient. Because little natural light reaches this area, a mixture of ambient and task lighting is required. The key feature here is the low-voltage halogen track light suspended from the ceiling of this recess. In addition, there are a couple of low-voltage, halogen desk lamps providing illumination for the whole of the work surface. The sparkling quality of the light is boosted by the clever extension of the blond-coloured, varnished, timber laminate flooring up the walls and across the ceiling of this work area. Once the working day is over, all these lights can be switched off and the recess recedes into the background.

❶ UP-FACING WALL LIGHTS   ❷ LOW-VOLTAGE HALOGEN PICTURE LIGHT   ❸ FLOOR-STANDING, LOW-VOLTAGE HALOGEN STANDARD LAMPS ❹ PENDANT LAMP   ❺ CEILING-SUSPENDED, LOW-VOLTAGE HALOGEN TRACK SYSTEM WITH DIRECTIONAL LAMPS ON LONG AND SHORT STEMS

A complex and flexible lighting scheme gives tremendous life and variety to this open-plan, loft living space. To make best use of the space, the lighting plan divides the room into different zones of activity. Each lighting circuit is controlled separately, making it possible to focus attention on just one area. In addition to the sitting and dining zones, the other main features are the storage units, one finished in rivetted metal panels,

the other painted blood red with a curved prow. On top of these two storage blocks are concealed low-voltage tungsten diachroic uplighters. Light bounces off the ceiling to provide a soft and relatively diffuse ambient lighting. The lighting is also designed to reinforce the presence of these blocks and enhances the sense of them 'floating' within the room. The floating illusion continues underneath the blocks with concealed Clickstrip edge lighting – flexible strips of xenon lamps. Light bounces off the polished maple floor surface, defining the bottom edge of the blocks. In the base of the red prow, a low-voltage light under an etched glass diffusing panel is activated automatically when the door is opened. A pair of spun-aluminium industrial drop lights are used over the etched glass table and provide low-glare pools of light over the translucent glass.

❶ CONCEALED LOW-VOLTAGE TUNGSTEN DIACHROIC UPLIGHTERS ARE FITTED ABOVE THE STORAGE UNITS

❷ CLICKSTRIP EDGE LIGHTING, FLEXIBLE STRIPS OF XENON LAMPS, BELOW THE UNITS

❸ ERCO SPUN-ALUMINIUM INDUSTRIAL DROP LIGHTS

cooking

THE HUB OF HOME LIFE, THE CONTEMPORARY kitchen has become one of the hardest-working rooms in the house. Along with its traditional role in storing, preparing and cooking food, it now embraces activities as diverse as laundry washing and ironing, family meals, children's homework, a home office, children's tea parties, the occasional bout of DIY, romantic suppers and even full-scale dinner parties. The primary concern is that it must work as a highly functional space, in which it is safe to prepare food and maybe also wash clothes, but, in addition, it must be capable occasionally of transforming into a more formal social space for entertaining.

Once out of sight and out of mind, tucked away in the basement or the back of the house, the kitchen today takes centre stage in home life. It is so thoroughly incorporated into our everyday activities that we can hardly imagine how it was once the sole domain of domestic staff and out of bounds for the family. To a Victorian householder, the very idea of eating in the kitchen would have been unthinkable; that we now invite our guests to share the space would be positively shocking. To effect the transformations from busy breakfasts to smart suppers, flexible and imaginative lighting design is the key.

assessing needs

CHECKLIST

Consider the following when planning your lighting scheme for the heart of the home:

- Is this an area used solely for food preparation and cooking?

- Is the room to be used for entertaining friends?

- Does it have to accommodate a range of different activities?

- Is it a designated room or part of a larger living space?

- Do you and your family eat here some or all of the time?

- Does it incorporate a home office?

- Is the decor generally light or dark in tone? Do you plan to change the scheme?

- Does it receive generous sunlight?

This single room provides the backdrop for a spectrum of activities, and that gives a clue to the approach for lighting. Imagine the room as a theatre set primed for everyday dramas – for the morning scene, it must be bright, cheerful and stimulating; as the day progresses, pools of light may be required over work counters for the preparation of meals; at dusk in winter the whole room may need to be lit up brightly for children's tea and homework, which then gives way to a softer mood for grown-up supper.

It is clear then that such a versatile space requires a sympathetic multi-functional lighting design. Think about the different scenes. At breakfast, the room will be at its brightest: a central pendant lamp over the table might be backed up by twinkling ceiling-recessed lights; there may be a track of ceiling-fixed spotlights highlighting a vase of flowers and reflecting light off kitchen cupboard doors; and to illuminate work areas, striplights hidden behind a baffle underneath wall-fixed cupboards and a couple of tiny lamps fitted into the extractor hood. This full-on scheme might also suit the homework and tea session after school. For food preparation, the track of spotlights and lights under the cupboard may suffice, while for a calm supper, focus attention on the centre of the room, with the pendant lamp and cupboard lights both on a low dimmer setting.

A really crisp lighting solution for a contemporary interior. Here a ceiling-fitted, single, low-voltage halogen track system provides more than a dozen light sources. Natural sunlight is drawn in through a roof light and a window adjacent to the eating area, and further illumination is provided for work areas by under-unit lighting.

lighting tips

We all take it for granted that there are electric lights inside a fridge, but seem entirely content to rummage around in unlit food cupboards. Consider fitting small lights inside cupboards, which are activated when you open the door. Alternatively, a ceiling-fixed track-lighting system could have its spotlights angled at those cupboards in most regular use.

Since you are thinking about a lighting system for the cooking area, this is also a good time to take the opportunity to add additional electrical sockets for kitchen equipment. Handy extra sockets can be fitted easily on the underside of kitchen wall cabinets – this way they are close to the work surface, yet invisible.

Demonstrating how lighting can powerfully affect the mood of a room. In this first shot of a three-picture sequence, the kitchen is shown in the morning lit entirely by natural sunlight.

SAFETY FEATURES

● Safety is paramount in the kitchen, so make sure that you do not prepare food while working in your own shadow – that is when accidents happen.

● Artificial light falling on work surfaces should come from just above and slightly in front of you.

● The same advice is true for cooker tops, hobs and sinks; make sure they are lit from above so that you can cook and wash up in absolute safety.

● Avoid trailing wires from lamps. A kitchen or cooking area is no place for table lamps.

The second mood is typical of a lighting style for early evening. Ceiling-recessed, low-voltage halogen lamps create scallops of light on the kitchen unit doors; some of this light is also reflected back into the room.

And finally, for later in the evening, providing a restful and intimate end-of-day setting, the lights are turned to almost their lowest setting using a dimmer switch. Lights by John Cullen Lighting.

bright ideas

We are often so intent on getting the lighting right for cooking and eating that the decorative potential of lights in the kitchen is forgotten. Some of the most stunning effects I've seen in recent years include those created by backlit panels. These can be simple but effective, either as whole sections of wall or as smaller panels behind a sink or work surface. The effect is achieved by fixing a sheet of glass or Perspex away from the wall and then inserting lights behind – slim tungsten or fluorescent tubes are best, but always make sure they are protected from excess heat or dampness. Consult your supplier – a sealed unit is preferred, and ensure there is easy access to change the bulb. Small points of light – tiny halogen spots or small fittings used in shop displays – inset into saucepan racks suspended over kitchen islands will provide drama and interest. These also provide practical illumination so that you do not have to work in your own shadow. If you want to mark out a dining area or breakfast bar, a really scintillating design solution is a lowered section of ceiling dotted with low-voltage halogen lamps.

Extremely elegant track-lighting, these flying-saucer shaped, low-voltage spotlights swivel on an axis, making it easy to direct light to exactly where it is required.

Directional lighting is particularly useful
in intensive work areas such as a
kitchen. This light fitting with its three
articulated heads on stems makes a
wonderfully flexible source of light for
the cooking area and work counter.

This is an extremely stylish lighting solution for the kitchen – a canopy of light suspended over a kitchen/dining area. The raft studded with low-voltage halogen spotlights adds real twinkle to the kitchen when it is at its brightest and, when dimmed, provides a soft, subtle glow.

This is a simple and unusual but highly effective lighting scheme to create visual excitement in the kitchen. This room is part of a basement area in a large house. It had been a sequence of rooms, but to improve the quality of the basement, the client employed an architect to open up the space, knocking together rooms and also opening the basement to the back garden. Materials were kept pale and simple with plain, off-white kitchen units, a pale timber floor and sparkling stainless steel details, including the wonderful cooker and hob and highly unusual triangular-shaped sink, which was designed by the architect and custom-made to fit the space.

Because this is in the lowest part of the house, artificial lighting was of utmost importance. There are three major lighting elements. The first and most eye-catching are the backlit splashbacks. These etched glass panels have been pulled forward from the wall by around 100mm and have ordinary fluorescent tube lighting fitted at the top. A useful design detail includes hinged access flaps in the cupboards above to make it easy to change the tubes. The glowing panels look absolutely fabulous at night when all other kitchen lighting is switched off.

1 FLUORESCENT STRIPLIGHTING BEHIND GLASS SPLASHBACKS THAT STAND PROUD OF THE WALLS **2** SMALL RECESSED HALOGEN LAMPS ILLUMINATING THE HOB **3** CEILING-RECESSED LOW-VOLTAGE HALOGEN LAMPS FOR OVERALL LIGHTING

The second area of fittings are the recessed lamps above the hob – these four lights provide really excellent light quality for cooking and create a nice sparkle washing down the white ceramic tiles of the splashback. The third lighting element are the ceiling-recessed lamps which provide washes of light down the front of the high-level kitchen units and create pools of light on the floor.

This spacious kitchen and dining extension has been designed to take advantage of natural sunlight. Roof lights over the food preparation area and over the dining table ensure that as much sunlight as possible is drawn into the room. And in the wall beside the dining table there are window slots to let in yet more light. Fins made using vertical oak timbers are placed at regular intervals along the wall to protect the room from the heat of intense sunlight. The space is beautifully finished with cream-coloured limestone flooring, neat honey-coloured timber kitchen units and a huge cast terrazzo work surface for the central island. The white colour scheme enhances the sense of light and space. The artificial lighting scheme has been designed with equal care and attention to every detail. Architectural tube lighting is used in the stainless-steel finished work area against the far wall. The upper line of tubes is hidden behind a baffle which sits below high-level cupboards. The second line of tubes has been fitted below a shelf so that you don't work in your own shadow. Recessed in the lowered ceiling above the island unit are three pairs of mains halogen lamps – these were chosen because the lamps operate without the need for transformers which makes the fittings cheaper, although the lamps themselves are slightly more expensive to replace. These lamps cast light directly on the stone work surface. In addition, there is a single line of mains halogen lamps recessed in the ceiling over the timber floor area which marks out the circulation route to the family sitting room.

① ARCHITECTURAL TUBES FITTED BEHIND BAFFLES AND BELOW A SHELF TO LIGHT WORK AREA   **②** PAIRS OF MAINS VOLTAGE HALOGEN LAMPS OVER STONE WORK SURFACE **③** LINE OF CEILING-RECESSED, MAINS-VOLTAGE HALOGEN LAMPS

din

dining

IN MOST HOMES THE DINING ROOM is an endangered space, if it has not already disappeared completely. As a result of our increasingly informal lifestyles, the whole ritual and ceremony of dining together as a family at three set times a day belongs to another era. New eating habits are considerably more fragmented than ever before. Breakfast, once a serious repast of meats, breads and dairy produce, has now been reduced to a snatched piece of toast or a quick visit to a snack bar on the way to work. Similarly, lunch at home has dwindled almost to insignificance. The working population no longer returns home for lunch with the family as many people are happy (or obliged) to grab a sandwich and get back to work. Even during the space of a generation, the traditional Sunday lunch has all but grown extinct. After school, children often prefer to eat snacks as they watch television to sitting at the table to eat, and plenty of adults, too tired at the end of the day or unable to cook, rely on convenience and takeaway food. However, for some, the one remaining vestige of the past is adult supper. When work is over and the day is done, many people still cook and eat a home-cooked supper, even if it is only a few times a week. It still remains part of our social life occasionally to invite friends and family to share supper sitting at the dining table.

Despite the enormous changes of the past few decades, most homes retain a dining table which becomes the focus of attention for entertaining and, when lit imaginatively, cannot fail to enhance the sense of occasion.

assessing needs

The dining room is the one place in the home that can be lit comfortably and successfully using candles alone, without any electric light. With this in mind, the best schemes are most likely to be the simplest. The dining area is usually simple, with the focus entirely on the tabletop. However, if the room includes interesting details such as a fireplace, paintings or display cabinets, highlight them with spotlights. In most cases, the soft, creamy light of a tungsten bulb is perfect for dining, while spotlighting has the option of either tungsten or the more twinkly halogen bulbs.

the lighting plan

Begin with a chandelier or pendant suspended over the table. This feature is often more decorative than functional and so, to boost general light levels, consider adding wall lights fitted with dimmers. These can be turned up to full brightness for informal occasions and down for more intimate suppers. A further option is a light raft or beam suspended over the table; bespoke versions can be designed to feature a mix of recessed uplighters and downlighters, operated by separate switches, to bounce light off the ceiling and cast it down on the table.

On the table itself, it is hard to beat eating by candle-light, produced by either a series of candlesticks or one large candelabra.

In a windowless room, three illuminated light boxes are used to create the sense of a sunbaked day outside. Fluorescent tube lights shine through turquoise plastic gel sheets, and wooden shutters can be adjusted to control the lightfall over a magnificent table, made to order, with real pebbles set in resin. The fluorescent lights are also on dimmer controls: when turned up it feels like a bright sunny day and when turned down it's a balmy evening.

Here the architect plays with daytime and night-time lighting to add interest in this large dining room. The pictures show the room lit with natural sunlight drawn into the room through a rectangular roof light. Harsh sunlight glare is kept at bay with the suspended glass panel which acts as a diffuser. At night, tube lighting fitted around the sides of the opening makes it glow like a light box. Once again the glass panel acts as a diffuser. At regularly spaced intervals around this feature are ceiling-recessed, low-voltage halogen lamps, and there are low-voltage halogen wall lamps. All sequences of lights are on different circuits and each is controlled by a dimmer switch.

practicalities

If your dining room or dining area is used during the daytime as well as the evening, consider installing two lighting schemes with different moods – something bright and uplifting for daytime and informal meals, and then a subtler, softer scheme for supper. Put each circuit or set of lights on a dimmer switch for maximum control and flexibility. This will allow you to light a serving area or sideboard when required, but will enable you to dim the area when you want to concentrate the light on the dining table for an evening supper.

If you choose a bright central pendant lamp, make sure it doesn't bounce harsh light off plates and the polished tabletop to dazzle your guests. If the height of your pendant or chandelier is adjustable, make sure it is not so low that it obscures the view across the table.

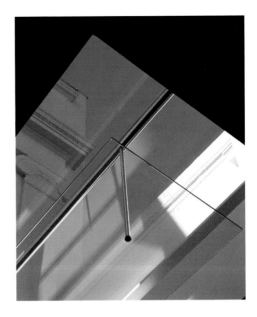

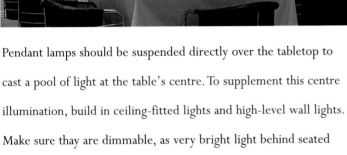

Pendant lamps should be suspended directly over the tabletop to cast a pool of light at the table's centre. To supplement this centre illumination, build in ceiling-fitted lights and high-level wall lights. Make sure thay are dimmable, as very bright light behind seated diners can produce odd shadows on the table.

If you do opt for a professional lighting designer, investigate the possibility of building in a control board with pre-set lighting programmes for different lighting schemes. It is even possible to programme light cycles that start, perhaps, with bright lighting early in the evening as people take their seats, and gradually become darker and more intimate as the evening progresses.

Finally, consider positioning pictures and wall lights slightly lower than you would in other areas of the house; this will be more comfortable and will prevent glare in guests' eyes as they are seated.

LIGHTING EFFECTS

The dining room is one place in the house well suited to drama, so there is plenty of scope for fantastic lighting.

● One sure way of making a dining room feel grand is to find a glittering chandelier or modern equivalent to act as a focal point and to cast a gentle, general light across the table.

● Along with a chandelier or similar, consider flamboyant wall lights and large, impressive candelabras.

● A pendant or chandelier lowered over the table will enhance the intimacy of dining with friends. Richly coloured walls and even a dark-painted ceiling will add to the effect.

● If you have a long table and choose to suspend a number of pendant lamps above it, choose an odd number of fittings – three, five or seven – as they are more aesthetically pleasing than even numbers.

● Because of their trailing flex, it is difficult to find electric lamps that sit comfortably and safely on a dining table. The option is to use candles which cast a welcome and flattering light with the added benefit of being a live, animated light source.

bright ideas

Preparing and sharing meals are among the highlights of any week. It is a wonderful time for bringing family and friends together and enjoying their conversation and company. Getting the atmosphere and surroundings right is just as important as spending time cooking, and lighting therefore plays an important role in the whole production. Great ideas can be borrowed from cafés and restaurants: look around at how the effects have been achieved, where lights are positioned and how many are used to illuminate each table or section of a restaurant. For breakfast and lunch an upbeat scheme is most appropriate – lots of bright light, preferably sunlight, to stimulate the senses and the taste-buds. In the evening, the more restful effect of candles is always a winner, but don't forget the potential of artificial lighting to add interest to the room – perhaps with an amazing splash of coloured neon, a panel of coloured, glowing light boxes, illuminated alcoves or a light fixture lowered over the table.

Light and glass are perfect companions. Here artifical lighting is used in an exciting way to transform this case of elegant glassware into a stunning framed artefact. The scheme is fairly complex, with downlighters fitted into the top of the cabinets to left and right and uplighters fitted in the middle cabinet. This adds great rhythm to the whole effect. In addition, outside the cabinet there are downward-facing spotlights in the ceiling which pick up the detail of the decorative cornice at the case top, as well as recessed uplighters at the foot of the two upright fascia boards which accentuate the vertical details. Lights by John Cullen Lighting.

A room with the simplicity and tranquillity of a monk's cell, this elegant dining space is conceived to provide a minimal, distraction-free backdrop to the serious pleasures of dining with family and friends. Key elements are the unadorned pale, but beautifully smooth, walls, the fireplace which has been reduced to a square void, the white blind to diffuse incoming sunlight and the broad timber planks for floor and table. The artifical lighting matches the scene perfectly and comprises lamps fitted at a low level behind the bench which runs along the fireplace wall. The bench acts as a baffle, so we don't actually see the light sources but can appreciate the almost ethereal glow, on the same level as the fire, as it washes up the wall.

A wonderfully light and spacious dining area in a contemporary-style home. The stripped-back style has been achieved through the use of simple but high-quality finishes and great artificial lighting. The pale-coloured timber floor adds a calm base to the interior, which is continued in the white walls. The clever panelling provides a sheer finish, but also disguises storage cupboards behind. There is just one vertical stack of open shelving. And despite this minimal approach with a limited palette of finishes, the space does not compromise on comfort. The circular dining table has a generous-sized top and the chairs are very comfortably upholstered. This dining area receives very little direct sunlight, but does benefit from indirect light flowing down the stairwell. The lighting scheme also contributes enormously to the elegance of the place. Ceiling-recessed, low-voltage halogen lamps cast a crisp downlight into the room and make pools of honey-coloured light on the floor. Attached to the beam which joins the white-painted column, there is a spotlight focussed on the vase of flowers. Additional illumination is provided by the unusual alcoves of light inset into the long storage wall. A high-level frame with a pair of tiny recessed spots is home to this trio of delicate sculptures.

❶ CEILING-RECESSED, LOW-VOLTAGE HALOGEN LAMPS ❷ TINY RECESSED SPOTS ILLUMINATE ORNAMENTS AND PLANTS IN RECESSED ALCOVES ❸ BEAM-FIXED SPOTLIGHT TRAINED ON THE DINING TABLE ❹ ILLUMINATED FISH TANK

There is a scattering of mid- and low-level alcoves along the stretch of wall that act as a frame for ornaments and plants. And perhaps one of the most eye-catching features is the lovely blue illuminated fish tank with its collection of fish and exquisite corals.

The mood is clearly upbeat in this open-plan living space with its sunny dining area. Natural sunlight is flooding in to the room through huge industrial -style windows. It cascades down the stairs uninterrupted by the neat glass-panel balustrading. In a contemporary interior of this sort lighting performs a number of functions – it is needed, of course, for general illumination at night, but can be manipulated to shape the space, create different moods and add points of interest. All of those objectives are met here. First, general ambient lighting is provided by the pair of simple, glowing pendant lamps on long-drop cables. The drop-shaped plastic case surrounds an ordinary tungsten light bulb and produces a warm and sunny yellow glowing light. For something a little cooler and sharper there's the ceiling-suspended low-voltage halogen track system. Here lamps are fitted on small movable arms to enable them to be directed to different parts of the room and pick out details. And finally, for intrigue, there are the coloured blue, yellow and white light boxes inset into the wall. Low-voltage halogen lamps have been recessed into the base of these sculpted boxes, making it impossible to see the actual source of light – but the intense light they shed on the painted back of the recess makes the opening appear to glow. The effect is intriguing in the daytime and quite stunning at night. The boxes are reminiscent of abstract paintings or small windows cut into the wall something like the famous Ronchamp Chapel designed by 20th century star architect Le Corbusier.

❶ PENDANT LAMPS ON LONG-DROP CABLES

❷ CEILING-SUSPENDED, LOW-VOLTAGE

HALOGEN TRACK LIGHTING WITH SWIVEL

HEADS FOR ADJUSTABLE FOCUS

❸ RECESSED LOW-VOLTAGE HALOGEN LAMPS

slee
sleeping

AS LIFE BECOMES MORE BUSY AND DEMANDING, bedrooms have assumed a vital role as havens of peace and tranquillity. Whether we want the uncluttered calm of minimalism or the reassuring cosiness of a more traditionally furnished room, the space must put us at ease. Many of the inspiring new ideas for improving bedrooms are drawn from hotel interiors where the emphasis is on making the most of sensual, natural materials such as sheepskin and suede, wood, deep pile rugs and gorgeous linen for sumptuous curtains or cool sheets. Pampering tops the agenda, with scented candles and aromatherapy oils used to create a calm atmosphere, and a return to rich woollen blankets, throws and quilted bedspreads.

However, while the room is associated largely with sleep, for most of us it is multi-functional: a place for storing clothes, dressing, applying make-up and drying hair, perhaps ironing, watching television, meditating, working out, even accommodating a home office. Equally tough demands are made by children, as their bedroom has evolved into a place for sleeping, homework, watching television, playing games and socialising. Also, importantly, it is where they can stamp their individuality.

Despite all these demands, the design of the bedroom has changed little during the past century, but is evidently poised for a make-over. Where there is the luxury of generous space, the bedroom is devoted solely to the bed with adjoining dressing room and bathroom. Where space is at a premium, the bed is a raised platform or foldaway unit, freeing up valuable floor space. Whatever the design of furniture and fittings, good lighting will give the space flexibility in use and mood.

assessing needs

CHECKLIST

To ensure your lighting scheme addresses all your requirements, consider the following points at the planning stage.

■ DO YOU HAVE A DRESSING TABLE AND MIRROR?

■ IS THERE A WASH-BASIN AND MIRROR?

■ IS THERE A FULL-LENGTH MIRROR?

■ DO YOU READ IN BED?

■ DO YOU USE THE ROOM FOR WORKING AT A DESK?

■ DO YOU SPEND A LOT OF TIME IN THE ROOM READING, OR SIMPLY USING IT AS A RESTFUL, PEACEFUL HAVEN?

Because we spend most of our time in the bedroom asleep, it is easy to think that this is a room where lighting is not important. But it is precisely because we use our bedrooms mostly when it is dark that well-planned artificial lighting is so crucial. Not only is it irritating and bad for your eyesight to read by a dim table lamp, it is also incredibly frustrating trying to find the right-coloured clothes in the dark recesses of a wardrobe.

the lighting plan

Bedrooms rarely tend to be huge or awkwardly shaped, so an average-sized double room, say 4 x 4m (12 x 12ft), could happily incorporate a basic scheme of a pendant lamp, a couple of table or reading lamps, and illumination for the wardrobe and/or dressing mirror. This provides a good start for most bedrooms, but if the décor includes dark furniture and rich, deep colours, supplementary lighting is recommended to add highlights to the colour scheme, perhaps in the form of extra wall lights and spotlights for pictures and architectural details.

But don't restrict yourself to the basics — there are plenty of opportunities in bedroom lighting to add character and drama to even the simplest rooms. A huge glittering chandelier will look equally stunning in a modern or period setting; high-level uplighters provide lovely soft light reflected off the ceiling; and twinkling, recessed halogen lights are great in alcoves illuminating paintings, sculptures or beautiful pieces of furniture.

Then there are the more practical considerations — wall-fixed, movable reading lamps are a great idea because they can be angled depending on whether you are sitting or lying in bed, and swung out of the way when not in use. Best of all are pairs of lights fitted

This simple but elegant sleeping platform, designed by Tonkin Architects, is lit by a basic, but entirely sufficient, ordinary dimmable light bulb in a ceramic holder. In addition, light rising from the floor softens the corners at the base of the platform.

SAFETY NOTE • SAFETY NOTE • SAFETY NOTE • SAFETY NOTE • SAFETY NOTE • SAFETY NOTE •

**FOR YOUNGER
CHILDREN IT IS
ADVISABLE TO BLOCK
OFF ACCESS TO ALL
ELECTRICAL SOCKETS
WITH DUMMY
COVERS.**

above the middle of a double bed where the light beams
point outwards – this allows one partner to sleep without
being troubled if the other light is switched on.

Lighting in wardrobes is an extremely good idea,
and not just at rail level so you can see your clothes, but
also at the lower level where you store shoes or smaller
items. Illumination close to dressing mirrors is a help, too,
although top lighting tends to be harsh, so you might try a more
flattering side light. Side lighting is also best for smaller mirrors. Just
like theatrical make-up mirrors, illumination is kindest when on all
four sides of the mirror, but adequate if just on the left and right.

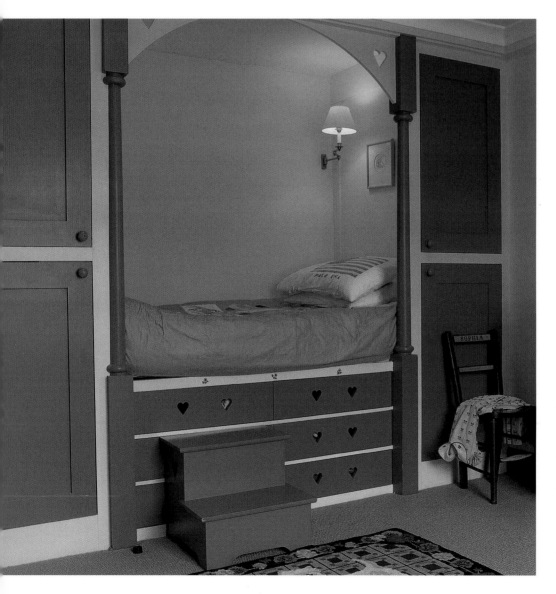

This cosy built-in
children's bed is
given a simple
wall-fixed lamp to
provide enough light
for reading bedtime
stories. Providing
general illumination
in the main part of
the room are ceiling-
recessed lamps.

practicalities

Getting the light-control switches right in a bedroom takes some care. Essentially, you will need to be able to switch on some or all of the lights at the door as you enter the room and then turn them off from the bed. When working on your lighting plan you need to know where the bed will be positioned so that you can decide where the switches will go. Also work out whether you need to control all the room lights from the bed or just the table lamps or reading lamps.

Another great idea, relatively new to the market, is the interior sensor light. Should you need to go to the bathroom at night, the sensors are activated by your movement and switch on a series of lights to illuminate your path, then turn them off when you go back to bed.

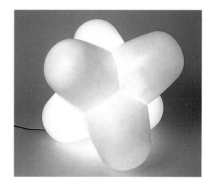

The brilliant Jacklight by designer Tom Dixon. This plastic moulded lamp is very tough and can be used just about anywhere. It is possible to stack them high and build an interlinked series of lights. Manufactured by Eurolounge.

children's rooms

Children's rooms have different needs from those of adults'. Children require generous light for playing safely and reading without eyestrain, but also some form of night-lighting. The best schemes incorporate a variety of fittings, which should be placed well out of reach and not include obvious dangers such as table and floor lamps which can be knocked over. One of the safest and most practical solutions is to use track lighting, where a series of lamps can be positioned to wash walls or cast light downwards for ambient lighting, while spotlights can be added to illuminate work areas.

Where the room is shared and children sleep in bunks it is a good idea to incorporate safe wall lights, where the bulb is protected by a cover, so that each child can control their own light.

Night-lights or lights controlled by dimmer switches are an extremely good idea for children of all ages – with babies a low level of illumination is useful for night-time feeding and nappy changing, while older children may find a degree of light reassuring in the middle of the night.

Intriguing linear strips of coloured light called Icon Long by designer Peter Christian and made by Aktiva. The light source is a T8 fluorescent tube and the lamp's colour derives from coloured gel inside the fitting. The variations in colour are made by different wattage lamps.

bright ideas

This restful space is enhanced by a thoughtful lighting scheme which makes the most of the room. Lights inside cupboards and wardrobes certainly qualify as bright ideas, as do lights for illuminating dressing mirrors. In addition, adjustable reading lights fixed to the wall win top points for practicality over the more traditional table lamps. They can be fitted exactly where the light is needed and there's no danger of knocking the lamp over or stumbling over trailing flex in the middle of the night. An idea for a sophisticated scheme is to do away with pendant lamps and use a couple of tall, floorstanding standard lamps or contemporary-style uplighters in room corners to reflect light off the ceiling. Standard lamps are so firmly associated with living rooms, it's easy to forget how good they can look in other spaces. You will be impressed with how the quality of diffuse light suits a bedroom.

A 'cloud' of lights hovers over the sleeping area of this angular and orderly living space. It brings a sense of intimacy and provides a practical solution to lighting in a building where the floors and ceilings are solid concrete. By making the cloud the right depth, recessed, low-voltage halogen lamps can be accommodated. Further light is added with the wall-fixed reading lamps which can be angled to where they are needed.

This pair of elegant, contemporary-style adjustable, wall-fixed reading lights is ideal for the bedroom. The articulated stems make it easy to move the light beam into precisely the right position for reading and the deep, cone-shaped shades focus the beam and prevent light spilling around the room. Wall-fixed lights are particularly useful in small bedrooms where there may not be room for lamps on cupboards or tables beside the bed. Also, being fixed to the wall, they are not in danger of being knocked over.

There's absolutely no reason why lighting design should lack wit and this simple design is a good example of wall lighting with a sense of fun. The Climbing Light designed by black+blum, with its spindly arms and legs, has instant appeal and still succeeds in being fairly practical. Its simple design includes a crown-silvered light bulb which contains the flow of light and directs it downwards and sideways, making it useful for reading. The on/off switch is trained to be easily accessible from the bed.

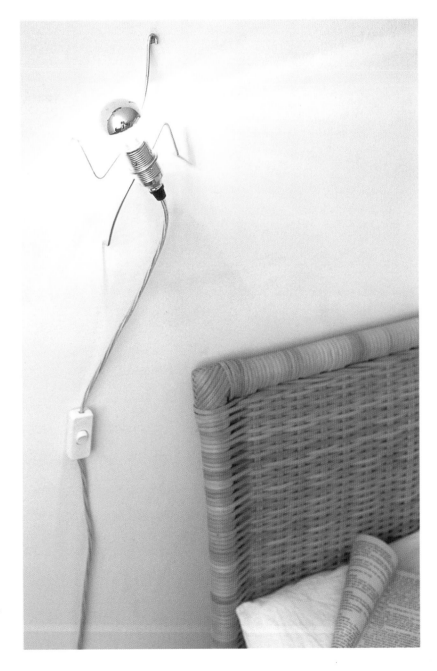

This crisp and calm bedroom interior is lit by blending a combination of light sources. There is upbeat background lighting, which is built upon with a wash upwards across the walls. To match the style of the room the fittings are understated and contemporary in design. The tone of the room is minimal and simple, there are no bright colours or pictures on the wall. Furniture is kept to a minimum too and finishes are plain and smooth. This space was designed for a city worker whose job entails considerable stress and pressure, and it's clear that here is a space for rest and recharging the batteries.

The room receives generous sunlight, with a whole wall-panel window situated at the foot of the bed facing west. The room is designed to enable some of this natural light to flood further in to the open-plan apartment. At the top of the wall behind and beside the bed are long horizontal slots of glass window through which the room receives generous sunlight. At night when the bedroom lights are switched on, these horizontal panels appear to glow when seen from the outside rooms.

The stars of the artificial lighting scheme are the strip of 'landing' lights set into the timber floor close to the wall. The upward beam of light reflects off the wall and flat-panel radiator and bounces into the room. The upbeams are unusual and distinctive and add intrigue to the otherwise simple room. On either side of the bed are wall-fixed reading lamps with adjustable 'gooseneck' stems.

❶ FLOOR-RECESSED, LOW-VOLTAGE TUNGSTEN DIACHROIC LIGHT FITTINGS

❷ INDIVIDUALLY SWITCHED, MAINS VOLTAGE TUNGSTEN DIACHROIC BEDSIDE LIGHTS ON ADJUSTABLE 'GOOSENECK' STEMS FROM AKTIVA

A combination of natural sunlight and artificial light succeeds in making the most of the generous sculptural shapes in this contemporary-style bedroom. The room is not large, but is given visual interest with the lovely curved sweep of wall and ceiling. These soft forms are ideal for a bedroom – they create a feeling of envelopment and protection, perhaps reminiscent, too, of a cave. Then there is drama and tension when the soft curve meets the flat ceiling. Here the room reverts to predictable geometric shapes. The furnishings are simple and restful. The bed headboard and small storage cupboards are built to fit the recess and are made as a single unit. The recess behind the bed is given emphasis and an interesting shadow effect by being painted a soft grey – the colour makes it clear that this area is set back from the rest of the room and frames the bed.

Natural light floods in through the square window which has been set on the outside face of the building; this design leaves a generous deep frame on the inside. The ceiling arches up and over towards the middle of the room, where it ends in a knife-edge sharp line before continuing as a flat ceiling. Along the entire length of this edge is a strip of tungsten tube lighting, composed of several tubes fitted end to end. This simple device immediately draws the eye and adds emphasis to the change of forms, the curling frozen-wave of wall and then the angular part of the room. At either side of the bed and fitted on the headboard is a pair of wall-fixed reading lights. These do away with the trailing cables of table lamps and are on movable arms which enable them to be swivelled into position. They are turned on and off with a simple pull cord.

Light is one of the most useful tools in giving shape and form to a space and here it is clear that the excitement of the room would be severely diminished without the inspired use of artificial lighting, and the highly unusual shape of this room is wonderfully quirky.

❶ TUNGSTEN TUBE LIGHTING FOR OVERALL ILLUMINATION

❷ CONTEMPORARY-STYLE WALL-FIXED READING LIGHTS ON ADJUSTABLE ARMS ALSO WITH WARM TUNGSTEN LAMPS

bathing

UNTIL RECENTLY THE BATHROOM HAS BEEN considered a highly functional space, a room dedicated exclusively to the necessary routines of washing and general hygiene. However, there is a whole new emphasis on the bathroom as a place for relaxation and renewal. It is now seen as a room for peace and privacy, away from the stresses of family, work and everyday life. The impact of the bathroom's new role can be measured by the amount of space we are prepared to devote to it. Many homes now incorporate en suite bathrooms, or perhaps separate bathrooms for adults and children. We are transforming spare bedrooms into extra bathrooms, building bathroom extensions or converting cellars into bathrooms which might also include a small home sauna or mini gym. There are even examples where bedrooms and bathrooms have merged into one to make an open-plan suite for rest and relaxation. Most frequently the lavatory has been separated out from the bathroom, leaving a space dedicated to washing, pampering, shaving, make-up and the general care we take in grooming ourselves.

Many of the most inspiring ideas for the home have been borrowed from hotel designs, where the luxuriousness of the bathroom has to match or even exceed that of the bedroom. These spaces incorporate ideas for spa baths, jacuzzis and amazing power showers, some of which double as water-massage units. Materials are chosen for their beauty in addition to their practical function, with marble, ceramics, glittering mosaic tiles and even glass wash-basins. Every corner is lavished with soaps, scented candles and soft towels. There may even be a music system, but there is *always* great lighting.

assessing needs

CHECKLIST

*We all use our bathrooms in
many different ways. Address the
questions below to ensure the
lighting meets your requirements:*

■ HOW IS THE ROOM
TO BE USED? (IE, FOR
QUICK GROOMING IN
THE MORNING, OR
FOR RELAXATION?)

■ HOW MANY PEOPLE
WILL THE BATHROOM
SERVE?

■ WHAT ARE THEIR AGES
– CHILDREN, YOUNG
ADULT, ELDERLY?

■ DOES ANYONE HAVE
RESTRICTED MOBILITY?

■ DO YOU NEED A BATH
AND A SHOWER?

■ DO YOU PLAN TO
EXPAND THE ROOM, ADD A
MINI GYM?

■ CAN YOU MAKE A
SEPARATE EN SUITE
WASHROOM TO RELIEVE
PRESSURE ON THE MAIN
ROOM AT BUSY TIMES?
EVEN A SEPARATE
WASH-BASIN IN A
BEDROOM CAN HELP.

■ IS THERE A LAVATORY
IN THE ROOM – IF SO,
DOES IT HAVE TO REMAIN?

The world can be divided into two types of bathroom user – those who like a quick, invigorating morning shower to freshen up and get on with the day, and those who want a long evening soak to read a book by candlelight, or to listen to the radio. To these there can be added a third category – children, who will want to play, splash water and have fun. All of this is fairly easy to accommodate where there is the luxury of more than one bathroom, but trying to combine these different uses in one room poses interesting design challenges. A flexible and imaginative lighting system can help enormously.

the lighting plan

Take account of the size, shape and décor of the space. There is no such thing as a typical bathroom, so look objectively at the space to be lit and start afresh with your plan. It is always advisable to build in flexibility by allowing for a generous number of light sources. As a general rule, unless your bathroom has incredibly high ceilings, it is wise to avoid pendant lights. Ceiling-recessed fittings tend to be a better option and sealed or waterproof units are best of all. They will provide plenty of ambient light while safely protecting bulbs from damp and any risk of water splashes. If the ceiling is unusually low, ceiling-recessed lamps are still a good

A subtle and clever lighting scheme where the rounded shapes of the bath and wash-basin are echoed in the large circular wall lights. The frosted, glass-domed covers create a pleasing diffuse light and protect the tungsten bulbs from the damp penetration inevitable in a steamy bathroom. Sparkle is added with ceiling-recessed low-voltage halogen lamps.

idea, but the illusion of extra height can be created through the use
of uplighters (either wall lights or perhaps strips fitted at the top of
cupboards) throwing light up onto the ceiling. Low-level lights,
fitted at skirting level below cupboards and casting light on the floor,
will also make a room seem higher. Make a virtue of a long, narrow
space by utilizing design features such as lamps recessed into the
floor — rather like an airstrip — or create the illusion of a wider

space by lining one long wall with mirrors to reflect both natural and artificial light back in to the room.

Consider colours and finishes also, as a bathroom is likely to be filled with highly reflective surfaces such as tiles, mirrors, stainless steel, marble and glass. To prevent harsh glare, consider lighting which can be reflected or softened with a baffle or panel of translucent glass. Where you do want real strength and visual accents, halogen lamps create wonderful sparkling light shining on glass shelving or glass bricks.

The bathroom is where you start and finish your day, so be kind to yourself and incorporate lighting which is bright enough for washing and grooming safely and comfortably, but not so bright or harsh that you illuminate every spot and wrinkle.

The best plans will provide good overall illumination, which is most successfully achieved with ceiling-recessed lamps, perhaps supplemented by wall lights. In addition, good illumination must be provided adjacent to the wash-basin and mirror. Here, take a tip from theatrical dressing rooms, where mirrors have lamps around all four sides, or, at the very least, down both sides. These will cast a clear, even light on your face. Ideally, the main room and mirror lights should be controlled independently of each other. I would also suggest a small light inside your medicine cupboard that switches on and off as the door is opened and closed, making it easy to read the small print on medicine bottles and packs.

With these basics in place, it is possible to add character and interest to the space with decorative lighting, positioned above and below cupboards, inset into walls or floors, or maybe even an illuminated panel of plain or coloured glass.

The beautiful elliptical Wedga wall light, made by Christopher Wray Lighting, is available in a white or brass finish and is a completely sealed unit, making it ideal for use in bathrooms.

An under-cupboard light designed for use in either the bathroom or kitchen. It uses a 12v capsule G4 10–20w max and is used where light is required on a surface below. From John Cullen Lighting.

This elegant, dark wood bathroom is filled with generous natural light coming through the sash windows. Artificial lighting includes the long striplight inset above the mirror, a trio of ceiling-recessed low-voltage halogen fittings, and the two large, industrial-style wall lights which illuminate the decorative cornice and bounce light off the ceiling.

PRACTICALITIES

Because water and electricity are a dangerous combination, bathroom lighting should be approached with enormous care.

● Light fittings including light and shaver socket units must be suitable for use in a damp atmosphere.

● Trailing cables are potentially very dangerous and should be avoided at all costs.

● The regulations governing electrical safety in the bathroom vary around the world. In the UK lights must be operated by a lightpull or a switch outside the bathroom, while in the US regular switches can be used inside. A qualified professional will be able to advise.

bright ideas

Inspiration here can be drawn from plenty of different sources. Nautical themes with porthole-style circular lights and domed bulkheads (lights with a wire grill often found on ships or outdoors) are always popular; however, with growing ranges of interesting external light fittings, it's worth looking at these more unlikely and unusual options. Square, circular and rectangular recessed lamps in walls, floors and ceilings are exciting, and so too are many of the contemporary-style designs intended for outside walls. Because exterior lamps are made as sealed units, they offer protection from bathroom damp. Also providing interesting effects are striplights hidden behind baffles; whether they are used above or below wall cupboards or at ankle level below floor cupboards, these strips of glowing illumination look great. They make cupboards appear to float in space, adding an ethereal quality to the room. Before buying any fittings and lamps for the bathroom, always check with your supplier to make sure they are appropriate for bathroom use.

Great lighting is the key to the high drama created in this small room. A low-voltage halogen lamp is fitted at the top of the recess behind the lavatory. It casts a bright beam of crisp light down through the glass shelves, over the pair of delicate porcelain vases and then on down to the large blue and white vase which sits on the lower shelf. Further low-voltage fittings are placed over a wash-basin to the right of the mirror to make the stainless steel basin and taps sparkle, and to light the mirror.

With so many toiletries now designed as beautiful objects of desire it seems a shame to hide them away in darkened cupboards. This idea is a true celebration of exquisite packaging and puts bubble baths, scents and creams in the spotlight. Rectangular recesses have been made in the bathroom wall at regular intervals and inside the hollowed case a small, sparkling halogen lamp is fitted in the top of the space to make a display case or frame for the toiletries.

Additional visual interest is added to this beautiful blue bathroom mosaic tilework with the inclusion of a couple of tiny, waterproof wall-fixed light fittings installed close to floor level. Because they are set in an unusual position, they are an intriguing feature in the room. The light they cast is reflected in the tiles and water. Some of the most interesting effects are created by using fittings in an unusual context or in an unexpected spot in the room.

An enticing contemporary bathroom that's a long way from the old-fashioned avocado-suite-and-tiles rooms of a generation ago. Here the style of room and lavish attention to detail demonstrate just how much emphasis we now place on the ritual and pleasures of bathing and relaxing and pampering ourselves in preparation for greeting the outside world. Exciting materials and great lighting combine to make a space that's uplifting and fun to use. Key details in the décor include tiny, off-white, floor-to-ceiling, mosaic wall tiles and lovely grey stone flags for the floor. But the star of the show must be the glass bricks. The pair of light columns flanking the wash-basin are an eyecatching feature – they draw the eye upwards and emphasise the height of the room as well as providing extra, soft, illumination. The panel of glass bricks makes a wonderful-looking and utterly practical shower enclosure.

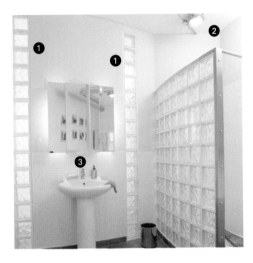

❶ SPOTLIGHTS ON THE EXTERIOR BACKLIGHT THE GLASS BRICK COLUMNS ❷ SEALED UNIT BULKHEAD FOR OVERHEAD ILLUMINATION ❸ SMALL SEALED-UNIT LAMPS BACKLIGHT THE MIRROR

The artificial lighting in this room comprises four main features. First and foremost are the columns of light which receive back illumination. Spotlights on the opposite side of the wall are positioned on the glass bricks and so produce a diffused light in the bathroom. Another element is the ceiling-fixed ndustrial-style bulkhead lamp. This lamp looks just as at home inside as it would on an outside wall. It is a sealed unit and so offers steam protection to the light bulb inside. There are also interesting small, sealed lamps fitted behind the mirrors which create a halo glow around the unit. Finally, and just out of this shot, there are ceiling-recessed lamps to illuminate the bath area.

The strong, simple geometric shapes and patterns of this bathroom have been given emphasis in the design of the lighting scheme, resulting in a warm, restful amosphere with a bold design twist. The centrepiece of this bathroom is the long, horizontal mirror-fronted cabinet which has the striking appearance of hovering in space. This effect is achieved by the inclusion of lighting tubes fitted both above and below the mirrored unit. Baffles are fitted so that the lamps are completely out of sight, and the light is reflected back in to the room rather than directly shining in. This gives a subtle glow, accentuated by the earthy tone of the walls, rather than the unflattering, harsh light so often found in bathrooms. The light is not just reflected close to the cabinet, but is also picked up in the shiny surfaces of the ceramic tiles, wash-basin and taps. The spread of the light is reduced above the cabinet where the ceramic tiles stop and the less reflective painted wall begins, giving the room depth and acting as a contrast to the light.

① TUNGSTEN TUBE LAMPS FITTED BEHIND BAFFLES ABOVE AND BELOW THE MAIN CABINET **②** CEILING-RECESSED LOW-VOLTAGE HALOGEN LAMPS, SPECIALLY DESIGNED FOR USE IN DAMP ATMOSPHERES

Additional lighting can be seen in the mirror reflection. A glass-fronted shower cubicle, which will reflect the light, can also be seen. General room lighting comes from the ceiling-recessed low-voltage halogen lamps – these are glass-fronted, sealed units specially designed for installation and use in the warm and damp atmosphere of a bathroom.

wor

working

EVERY YEAR GROWING NUMBERS OF US are giving up commuting, canteens and office gossip in exchange for working at home. It can be one of the best moves you will make in life, allowing you to take control of your time, your workload, and your work environment. But if you want to earn a living, setting up an office at home is no soft option. It requires discipline and self-sufficiency to work alone for days at a time.

One of the keys to success is to make sure your home office is a welcoming and inspiring place, where it is genuinely enjoyable to work. It doesn't have to occupy a huge amount of space, but if you take your job seriously, you must take your office seriously. Don't think you can get by perching on the edge of a table. The temptation in the past has been to relegate an office to a far-flung corner of the home – we may feel that if the computer is out of sight it will also be out of mind. But increasingly, there is more emphasis on creating a high-quality environment.

The classic home office location is in the guest bedroom. If you have the luxury of this extra space, it makes excellent use of a room that is otherwise almost certainly under-used. If it is in a house, the bedroom is likely to be on an upper floor and therefore blessed with good natural light, views, and separation from general family noise and disturbance. However, where space is at a premium think about setting up your desk in a regularly used bedroom where at least it is quiet during the day. Take over the corner of a living room or consider investing in converting an attic or even building an extension. Both of the latter ideas will make a useful office and add value to your property.

assessing needs

CHECKLIST

Think carefully about your office needs before planning the space and its lighting. Here are some points for consideration.

■ CAN YOUR WORK BE ACCOMPLISHED IN A SMALL SPACE, OR DO YOU NEED ROOM TO SPREAD OUT?

■ CAN YOU WORK WHERE THERE IS GOOD NATURAL LIGHT?

■ IS IT POSSIBLE TO ADD OR ENLARGE A WINDOW TO BRING IN MORE NATURAL LIGHT?

■ A GOOD DESK LAMP IS INVALUABLE. IT IS WORTH SPENDING EXTRA ON A LAMP WITH A HEAVY BASE, WHICH CAN BE ANGLED TO CAST LIGHT PRECISELY WHERE IT IS NEEDED

The quality of your work space will be affected by light. Natural light makes a comfortable environment, but it will need to be supplemented by an artificial lighting scheme. The primary function of good office lighting is to create a comfortable and stimulating work space. It must be possible to see clearly, without eyestrain and without glare. To achieve this, general lighting levels must be higher than elsewhere in the home. For concentrating on detailed, close-up and complex work we need more light still, and the older we get the more light we need to see accurately. It is worth noting here that poor lighting will not just affect emotions and performance at work, it can also have an adverse physical effect. Inadequate lighting will cause eyestrain, which in turn can provoke tense neck and shoulder muscles and headaches.

natural light

Natural daylight provides the most comfortable illumination for working in. With the exception of very dull, overcast days, it is a great deal brighter than artificial lighting, and it also has the great advantage of being an even light, free from hot spots of glare. Because our bodies are sensitive to light, we are stimulated by high levels of illumination and so the ideal home office will have large windows, skylights or French doors to allow in the maximum natural lightfall. Where natural light levels are low, it is worth considering enlarging or even adding windows. In the northern hemisphere, rooms with north-facing windows provide a cool, even light. Those facing south will receive the full force of the sun, so you will need to hang blinds of some sort to diffuse the light and stop heat building up. East-facing openings get bright light in the mornings, and those facing west will be at their brightest in afternoons – this can cause dazzle on computer screens, so angle them away from direct sunlight, ensuring your eyes are always comfortable when working.

Useful for occasional short bursts of computer work, this long corridor work area is painted with strong vibrant red and features a sculpted work surface. Natural light flows into the space from either end of the corridor and also through the unusual horizontal window at ankle level. Artificial lighting is provided by a simple wall light over the work area.

the lighting plan

The scheme in a home office should be based around providing good all-round, ambient lighting plus boosters in the form of desk lamps and spots for close-up work. The contrast between ambient and task lighting should not be too dramatic as this causes eyestrain.

A basic scheme for a small room might include a central pendant light plus a couple of desk lamps. However, it is likely that this will leave areas of the space in shadow – incredibly frustrating if you are trying to find something. To counteract this, add a ceiling- or wall-mounted track of three or more fittings close to the work area to provide spotlighting for specific features, such as a bookshelf, or to highlight a painting. These can also be angled at the ceiling and walls to bounce light around the room. Alternatively, consider floor-standing uplighters or wall lights, both of which will cast light on the ceiling. Commercial office furniture stores are excellent sources of useful lighting, including impressive, tall, freestanding lamps that cast light down over a work surface as well as up at the ceiling. Although expensive, these can be plugged in to an ordinary electrical socket, avoiding the need for a professional fitter.

Called the Flexilight, this elegant adjustable lamp is ideal for use in a home office. It has a shiny chrome finish and a low-voltage halogen lamp and is produced by Aktiva. It is also available in a mains lamp version.

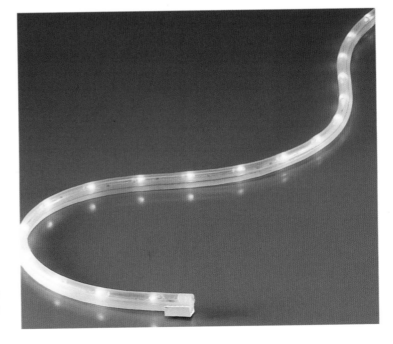

This string of tiny bulbs known as a Lightstream is flexible and small enough to be fitted in the most awkward spaces. It comes complete with fixed 230v or 12v integral lamps, 28w per metre, which are concealed in a flexible, sealed, clear silicone sleeve. The average life of this product is an incredibly impressive 20,000 hours. From John Cullen Lighting.

Where your home office is in a dual-purpose room, perhaps a living room or guest bedroom, lighting can be used to amazing effect to define the space and mark boundaries. For example, a line of ceiling-recessed low-voltage halogen lights above the work area will highlight just that part of a room when it is in use.

Here is a room blessed with great natural sunlight, and the lavish use of timber makes this a warm and inviting interior. On the mezzanine level is a small home office which receives plenty of natural light from the large window and benefits from the big industrial-style downlighters fitted snugly into the roof's apex.

practicalities

One of the great problems in lighting a home office is to make sure you avoid glare and shadow. Desk lamps are best placed at the side of the computer to prevent them from casting light on the screen. It is also a good idea to have a light at the back of the desk that casts illumination over the keyboard and phone, so you can work without being plunged into your own shadow.

bright ideas

Work areas such as home offices need practical schemes producing high levels of natural and artificial lighting, but functionality doesn't have to rule out fun or finesse. It is widely acknowledged that lighting levels can affect our performance, so one or two extra lamps for dull days are a great idea. It's a great spirit-lifter and positive influence to have a lamp or fitting in your work area which is either a very beautiful design – perhaps a really elegant floor or desk lamp – or something which makes you smile – a lamp in the shape of a duck, the Eiffel Tower, or whatever takes your fancy. Invest in a couple of floor-standing uplighters to provide extra diffused light bounced off the ceiling, and always take a look at office furniture stores where some of the smartest lighting designs are on offer. One recent innovation has been floor-standing lamps which cast light downwards on the desk top as well as upwards onto the ceiling for a diffused light. These are expensive, but quite wonderful. Bright ideas might also include a crystal block lamp where a bulb is set inside a block of real salt crystal. The belief is that the salt absorbs impurities from the air, particularly around computer equipment.

Charming and elegant, these Oskar bookshelf lights, designed by lighting design guru Ingo Maurer, are destined to become real classics. The ingenious design makes it easy to slot them in between the books and then bend the stainless steel gooseneck stem so that light falls onto the spines.

This is a subtle and clever scheme for a typically small home office area. The space, at the top of a stair, receives no direct natural light, but to help counteract this, has been painted white and kept fairly clutter-free to reflect the artificial lighting. In an area such as this, where there is so little or no natural sunlight, it is an extremely good idea to keep walls free of paintings or pinboards, as any dark or matt surfaces will absorb light and make it appear yet darker. The artificial light can wash over the walls unbroken, making the most of the lighting scheme and minimising unwanted shadows. Additionally, this opens up the area, giving the appearance of more space than there actually is. This thoughtful scheme features just one small image of a book and the striped wall hanging.

The lighting scheme comprises several elements. There is a ceiling-fixed track of low-voltage halogen spotlights over the desk to provide general ambient lighting in the space. This is boosted with a very bright, low-voltage halogen task lamp on the desk which is directed right over the work area. The combination of these two light sources ensures that the work area is always comfortably lit, and you are never working in your own shadow. There is a further halogen light fitting to the right of the space and suspended over the stairwell – this double lamp fitting has one beam of light directed into the work area and one skimming down the unusual framed, skinny-rib dress on the wall. At the base of the half-height wall which wraps around the desk area is a small recessed, ankle-level light which marks the top of the stairs, providing both a practical safety feature and an unusual light source.

1 CEILING-SUSPENDED, LOW-VOLTAGE HALOGEN TRACK FOR GENERAL AMBIENT LIGHT **2** LOW-VOLTAGE HALOGEN DESK LAMP FOR DIRECT LIGHT ON THE WORK AREA **3** LOW-VOLTAGE HALOGEN DOUBLE LAMP FITTING OVER THE STAIRWELL **4** RECESSED FITTING WITH TUNGSTEN LAMP.

outside

NOT ONLY DO OUR GARDENS AND outdoor spaces look quite different from a few years ago, but we are also using these areas in different ways. We have moved on from the traditional lawn surrounded by borders, enjoyed for just a couple of weeks in summer, to a garden which is now seen as an extension of the home, an outdoor room that we want to use as often as possible. Recent surveys have shown that while a small number of people still regard gardening as a hobby, the rest of us see it as a chore and want to be out in the garden having fun without putting in backbreaking work. In response to these new demands designers have been hard at work devising contemporary-style, low-maintenance schemes where water features and sculpture take precedence over the prize petunias, and where a dining table and chairs are just as important as the pot plants. An entire industry has sprung up to help us make the most of even the tiniest terraces. There are endless new ranges of beautiful outdoor furniture, thousands of barbecues and garden ovens, decking materials, automatic, computer-controlled watering systems and café-style heaters that make it possible to sit out and have a drink with friends even in the winter.

Another major tool in making it possible to extend and enhance the time spent in the garden is artificial lighting. The most creative schemes will not just illuminate the space when we are in it, but will also make it stunning to look at from inside the home.

assessing needs

CHECKLIST

Garden lighting schemes are a fairly new concept; to help your planning, here are some points to consider

■ DO YOU HAVE INTERESTING PLANTS OR FEATURES IN THE GARDEN THAT YOU WOULD LIKE TO HIGHLIGHT?

■ ARE YOU THINKING OF ADDING A WATER FEATURE? ILLUMINATED WATER CAN BE EXTREMELY ATTRACTIVE.

■ IS THERE A WALL OR FENCE CLOSE TO THE DINING AREA WHERE LIGHTS CAN BE FIXED?

■ IF PEOPLE ARE LIKELY TO WALK THROUGH THE GARDEN, CONSIDER ADDING SOLAR-POWERED, GROUND-LEVEL LAMPS TO MAKE IT SAFE TO NEGOTIATE.

■ CAN YOU ADD DEPTH AND INTEREST TO THE GARDEN BY ILLUMINATING TREES OR A FEATURE PLANT AT THE FAR END?

Before embarking on your outdoor lighting plan, take time to consider seriously what you want to achieve and, very importantly, how much you are prepared to spend. Introducing a full lighting scheme to a garden can be a very expensive enterprise, but there are plenty of alternatives that will enable you to light small areas beautifully, for little outlay. The first point to remember is that night-time lighting should be subtle – it is quite unnecessary and unappealing to attempt to illuminate an entire garden.

lighting style

Light fittings for the garden used to be rather municipal in style, with interesting fittings hard to find, but with the growing interest in the garden as an 'outdoor room' has come a huge choice of great fittings. There is now everything from the traditional, durable bulkheads for lighting paths and walls to clever solar-powered lights on stalks which, because they need no wiring, can be moved around the garden as required. Other new eye-catching designs include plastic-cased lanterns on a string that can be hung around a dining terrace; a vast choice of all-weather spotlights; underwater light fittings; table pendants; wall lights and adjustable fascia lights – the latter are the type of lamps used to illuminate shop fronts, but are ideal for washing garden walls with light.

Cloister-like abstract frames are pulled forward of the garden wall and then tube lights are slotted into the inner rims to define the sharp edges of the frames. The light is reflected off the blue wall behind. For safe navigation of the poolside path there are ankle-level lamps fixed to the wall. Their capped tops ensure that light is directed downwards at the path and not upwards to dazzle anyone walking by.

the lighting plan

A large part of the charm of being outside at night is the magic of the darkness, and the best design schemes are careful to respect that. To create a restful atmosphere, powerful searchlights and spotlights should be avoided. Since a table is likely to be the focus of any evening use of the garden, this is the starting point of a lighting design scheme. The idea here is to mark the boundaries with light, illuminate the table top and perhaps provide some additional feature lighting on the terrace or deck. Where the budget is modest and the table is close to the house, lighting in the form of strings of lights or lanterns (always checking they are intended for exterior use) can be plugged into indoor sockets and then hung around the perimeter of the dining area or balcony. Additional lighting might include hurricane lamps on the table using candles, battery power or a burning spirit such as paraffin.

For an old-fashioned look, this low-level newel-post lamp comes with shatter-proof glass – very important if children play in the garden. Called the Ludgate, it is ideal for lighting pathways and is from Christopher Wray Lighting.

Where the dining table is under cover, perhaps in an open-sided marquee or covered arbour, the structure may provide a useful frame for permanent electric cabling – of course, this must be the outdoor variety, with protective coating against the worst weather. With this in place there's an opportunity to suspend pendant lamps over the table. As before, keep the light levels low.

For a more contemporary look, here is a chunky exterior, silver-finished, metal wall light. It is called the Domino and is also by Christopher Wray.

To make it easy and safe to navigate the garden, pathway illumination is a good idea. This can be achieved cheaply and dramatically with flame torches, which can be bought from most garden centres, or perhaps a series of candle lanterns on the ground or hanging from poles lining the path. An electric scheme might include low-level lamps just a few centimetres off the ground and installed at the sides of the path. The fittings cannot be seen and the light is cast across the path without glare. If the path runs alongside a wall, consider fitting bulkheads. For flights of stairs, fittings can be recessed into the sides of steps.

safety

A full lighting scheme requires the garden to be wired in a similar way to the wiring of a room inside the house. It is advisable to use accredited professionals who will specify the correct exterior grade of cabling and will know how and where it is to be installed, to avoid damage by gardening equipment such as lawnmowers and spades.

security features

Exterior lighting is often part of a home's security system. Most common are sensor lights, which are switched off most of the time and only activated by movement or heat. These are best fitted by security system experts and should be on an entirely different electrical circuit from any other outdoor lighting.

Light and moving water make a mesmerising combination. The clever scheme here makes good use of underwater lamps shining up through low-level fountains. As a backdrop there's a cascade of water between the tall standing stones which also receives light from below the surface of the pool. The uplighting is sufficiently powerful also to illuminate the overhanging tree.

bright ideas

In the garden, the best ideas are almost always the simplest. A path lined with large garden flares dug into the ground can look incredibly handsome; candles on tables are also an extremely welcome sight. There's something about moving flame which seems to appeal to us all. Tiny tea-light candles in a line of jam jars edging a terrace or path look fabulous. Strings of exterior lights bought for Christmas decorations can make a summer appearance hung around a terrace or deck, and electric or solar-powered uplights on short stems always look stunning dug into the bottom of a bush or long grass.

There are few things to beat the beauty of real moving flames at night and outdoors. This stepped timber walkway is made incredibly grand with the addition of flanking garden torches that flare in the night breeze.

While we are accustomed to seeing sculpture outdoors, the idea of hanging pictures in the garden is highly unusual. However, this timber terrace has tremendous style with its pictures and trellis picked out by small all-weather spotlights. The pictures are protected in weather proof frames.

A lovely tangle of grasses sit in a galvanised trough against a cream-painted wall topped by horizontal slatted fencing. The lighting brings out the visual interest of all these textures. Three equally spaced small spotlights (Maxispotters) fixed on the fence cast neat cones of light down across the timber and into the grasses. Meanwhile a ground-level spot, just out of the picture on the left, lights up through the grasses, casting interesting shadows on the wall behind. To add yet more interest, lamps (Reflecteur Jardins) are also planted in the trough and cast light upwards. Lights by John Cullen Lighting.

Because the garden has now become an extension of our indoor living space, in which we often spend the majority of our time when the weather is good, it's importance has grown to such an extent that it is common for gardens to be wired with as many fittings and sockets as any indoor room. However, there is a great deal to be said in praise of a subtle and thoughtful approach. The mystery and magic of evenings spent out of doors would be completely lost, the ambience spoilt, if the space was illuminated to daytime levels. The fun in designing an exterior scheme is in making interesting pools of light, points of interest dotted around the garden, while also creating a focus of attention – usually a table or other outdoor furniture.

In this case, the densely grown town garden has a table and chairs on a terrace and is surrounded by just a couple of pools of light. Starting with the table, a soft dining light is provided by the pair of candles in their glass storm lanterns. Then, very cleverly, a small spot of light is directed at the vase of summer flowers in the table's centre – this spotlight is fixed up above the table to the tree behind. Just in front of the table and near ground level on the left another spot is pointed upwards to light some of the greenery, providing interest and enhancing the outdoor feeling. Extra depth is created with a further couple of upward facing spots in the middle and far distance on the left-hand side, lighting the terracotta pots and the intriguing iron frame with its spherical frame on top.

❶ A SPOT JARDIN WALL (EXTERNAL, DIRECTIONAL, WALL-MOUNTED, LOW-VOLTAGE SPOTLIGHT) ❷ REFLECTEUR JARDINS CREATE POOLS OF LIGHT ON SHRUBBERY ❸ SPOT JARDINS (GREEN COMPACT SPOTS WITH GROUND SPIKES) CREATE UPLIGHTING. ALL FROM JOHN CULLEN LIGHTING

Artificial lighting can add an extra dimension to any garden and extend its use and appeal through the evening hours. And the incorporation of a lighting scheme is just as important in a small garden as it is in a large one. In this town garden, by British designer Jill Billington, the planting is on ground and basement levels linked by the handsome metal spiral staircase. The whole area is enclosed by lovely old brick walls, which blend with the plants and provide a solid base for lighting fixtures. In the daytime, the upper-level space receives a great deal more natural sunlight than it does below, so the basement area shown is lavishly planted with

plants which enjoy or tolerate shade, including clematis, ferns, clipped box and a Japanese anemone. Views of this rich, dense foliage are enjoyed from the basement kitchen. Among the main design elements is the water feature, which begins on the upper level as a mini canal and then flows to the lower level by sliding down this piece of slate. The idea was to add movement to the garden, but to keep the noise of water to a subtle minimum. The lighting scheme makes much of the feature and includes an underwater spotlight at the base of the waterfall to uplight the piece of slate, creating a very dramatic night-time effect, while at the top of the slate there is a wall-fixed outdoor spotlight illuminating a bas-relief sculpture on the higher

❶ FULLY, SEALED, UNDERWATER SPOTLIGHT FIXED AT THE BASE OF SMALL WATERFALL TO UPLIGHT THE FLOWING WATER ❷ WALL-FIXED, SEALED, EXTERIOR WALL LIGHT TO HIGHLIGHT A PIECE OF GARDEN SCULPTURE ❸ SEALED, EXTERIOR SPOTLIGHTS WITH GROUND SPIKES TO CREATE UPLIGHTING THROUGH FOLIAGE

level. At intervals around the garden and interspersed between the dense planting there are further spotlights, hidden from view but providing light to illuminate the plants.

architects

A selection of architects and designers whose projects are featured in this book

Allford Hall Monaghan Morris
5 Old Street
London EC1
Tel: 020 7251 5261
page 50

The Architects Practice
23 Beacon Hill
London N7
Tel: 020 7607 3333
page 49

Belsize Architects
48 Parkhill Road
London NW3
Tel: 020 7482 4420
*pages 38, 39, 46, 78,
79, 109*

Jill Billington
Tel: 020 8886 0898
pages 138–9

Hugh Broughton
4 Addison Bridge Place
London W14
Tel: 020 7602 8840
page 106

Neil Choudhury
132 Southwark Street
London SE1
Tel: 020 7633 9933
pages 35, 105

Form Design Architecture
1 Bermondsey Exchange,
179-181 Bermondsey Street,
London SE1
Tel: 020 7407 3336
pages 58–9, 98–9

KDA Stair Design
Tel: 020 8806 8399
page 77

LGH Architects
12 Chelsea Wharf,
London SW10
Tel: 020 7351 7871
pages 70–1

Project Orange
116 Golden Lane
London EC1
Tel: 020 7689 3456
pages 72–3, 100–1, 114–15

Studio MG
101 Turnmill Street
London EC1
Tel: 020 7251 2648
page 95

Tonkin Architects
24 Rosebery Avenue
London EC1
Tel: 020 7837 6255
page 91

designers & stockists

Aero
96 Westbourne Grove
London W2
Tel: 020 7221 1950
Range of contemporary-style
furniture and lamps

After Noah
121 Upper Street
London N1
Tel: 020 7359 4281
Home décor shop; also stocks unusual
second-hand lighting

Aktiva
10b Spring Place
London NW5
Tel: 020 7428 9325
info@aktiva.co.uk
www.aktiva.co.uk
Producers of low-voltage, modern light fittings

Aram Designs
3 Kean Street
London WC2
Tel: 020 7240 3933
Range of high-quality contemporary
designs, furniture and lighting

Aria
133 Upper Street
London N1
Tel: 020 7226 1021
Contemporary interior design
shop with lighting

Artemide
323 City Road
London EC1
Tel: 020 7833 1755
Renowned Italian lighting designer
and manufacturer

Atrium
Centrepoint
22–24 St Giles High Street
London WC2
Tel: 020 7379 7288
Contemporary interior design shop
with lighting, including modern classics

Babylon Design
Unit 7 New Inn Square
1 New Inn Street
London EC2
Tel: 020 7729 3321
Lights by adventurous contemporary designers

Ball
177 Waller Road
London SE14
Tel: 020 7635 8792
www.studioball.co.uk.
Amazing wild designs mixing art and design

black+blum
2.07 Oxo Tower Wharf
Barge House Street
London SE1
Tel: 020 7385 4216
design@black–blum.com
www.black–blum.com
Unusual contemporary designs

Box Products
The Lodge
3 Russell House
Cambridge Street, London SW1
Tel: 020 7976 6791
Box-designed products and bespoke design service

Central
33–35 Little Clarendon Street
Oxford OX1
Tel: 01865 311141
Interiors shop with lighting section

Christopher Wray Lighting
Main Showroom
600 King's Road
London SW6
and 18 branches around the UK
Tel: 020 7751 8701
Fax: 020 7751 8699
www.christopher-wray.com
Lights, shades and lighting accessories
in a variety of styles from traditional to modern

Co-Existence
288 Upper Street
London N1
Tel: 020 7354 8817
Contemporary furniture and fittings

Conran Shop
Michelin House
81 Fulham Road
London SW3
Tel: 020 7589 7401
Range of contemporary lighting

Cotterels Lighting
28–35 Carnhouse Place
Glasgow
Tel: 0141 225 2888
Good selection of contemporary designs

Cowley Designs
Clifton Road
Blackpool
Lancashire FY4
Tel: 01253 831500
Warehouse supplying wide range of interior
goods including lighting

Creative Element
2 King Lane
Clitheroe
Lancashire BB7
Tel: 01200 427313
Contemporary interior design
including lighting

The Design Shop
10 Richmond Hill
Richmond
Surrey TW10
Tel: 020 8241 2421
Contemporary interiors including lighting

El Ultimo Gritto
26 Northfield House
Frensham Street
London SE15
Tel: 020 7732 6614
Contemporary designers

Erco
38 Dover Street
London W1
Tel: 020 7408 0320
Leading manufacturer of high-quality
light fittings, highly favoured by architects

Flos
31 Lisson Grove
London NW1
Tel: 020 7258 0600
Great range of contemporary fittings

Habitat
Tel: 0645 334433 for nearest store
Selection of contemporary domestic
lights and fittings

Ikea
Tel: 020 8208 5600 for nearest store
Range of good value, contemporary
domestic lamps

Inflate
11 Northburgh Street
London EC1
Tel: 020 7251 5453
Innovative designers of furniture and lighting

John Cullen Lighting
585 King's Road
London SW6
Tel: 020 7371 5400
Fax: 020 7371 7799
Designers and makers of contemporary
fittings for all applications

John Lewis
Oxford Street
London W1
Tel: 020 7629 7711
Mix of traditional and modern styles

The London Lighting Company
135 Fulham Road
London SW3
Tel: 020 7589 3612
Wide choice of contemporary lighting designs

Jeremy Lord
The Colour Light Company
Unit 28 Riverside Business Centre
Victoria Street
High Wycombe Buckinghamshire
Tel: 01494 462112
Designer of extraordinary installations
including the multi-coloured Chromawall

Mathmos
20–24 Old Street
London EC1
Tel: 020 7549 2743
Famous for the lava lamp, but there's
more besides

Ingo Maurer
Kaiserstrasse 47
80801 Munich
Germany
Tel: 0049 89 381 6060
www.ingo-maurer.com
Amazingly inventive designer of
contemporary lighting

New Rooms
51 High Street
Cheltenham
Gloucestershire
Tel: 01242 2379777
Contemporary interior designs including lighting

Purves & Purves
220-224 Tottenham Court Road
London W1
Tel: 020 7580 8223
Wide range of modern furniture and lamps

Ralph Capper Interiors
10a Little Peter Street
Manchester M16
Tel: 0161 236 6929
Contemporary furniture and lighting

SCP
135–139 Curtain Road
London EC2
Tel: 020 7739 1869
(Also at Selfridges' fourth floor contemporary
furniture concession) contemporary furniture
and lighting

Selfridges
Oxford Street
London W1
Tel: 020 7629 1234
Department store with strong lighting department
showing lots of contemporary designs

Set Design
100 High Street
Leicester LE1
Tel: 0116 251 0161
Contemporary furnishings including
great Italian lighting

SKK
34 Lexington Street
London W1
Tel: 020 7434 4095
Wild stuff from innovative lighting
designer Shiu Kay Khan

Topen Design
Saddlers Court
Perthshire PH14
Tel: 01828 626176
www.topendesign.co.uk
Innovative and modern lights and light fittings

Viaduct Furniture
1–10 Summers Street
London EC1
Tel: 020 7278 8456
Chic contemporary lamps

Jo Whiting
32 Laurel Avenue
Twickenham
London TW1A
Tel: 020 8891 2344

index

picture credits